Lowell Branning
1937

BAND—AT-TEN-TION!

BAND — AT-TEN-TION!

A Manual for the Marching Band

BY

MARK H. HINDSLEY

DRILL MASTERS AND
DRUM MAJORS EDITION

GAMBLE HINGED MUSIC CO.
CHICAGO, ILLINOIS

To the memory of

GROVER C. CLEAVER, CAPT., U. S. A.

and to those

INDIANA UNIVERSITY BANDS
OF 1924 TO 1929

*of which he was the inspirational drillmaster
this book is dedicated*

PREFACE

"Band—At-ten-tion!" has been published as the result of a widespread appreciation of Mr. Hindsley's success with school marching bands. His outstanding accomplishment with the Heights High School Band at the National Music Supervisors Conference, Cleveland, 1932, has focused upon his work the interest of the band profession.

Mr. Hindsley's experience as musical director of the Indiana University Band from 1924 to 1929, followed by three years directing and drilling the Heights High School Band has given him an appreciation of the problems confronting all directors and drillmasters.

While the military phase of marching evolutions is essential, the author has co-ordinated it with the musical side in a way that meets the enthusiastic approval of musical directors. The style is clear and concise, making previous military experience unnecessary. Complete and in logical order, the material is invaluable for bands wishing a full training program.

Should you question the value of taking time to develop your playing band into a marching band, you will find a most convincing answer in the Introduction to this book, reprinted from Music Supervisors Journal, December, 1930, issue.

THE PUBLISHERS.

AUTHOR'S FOREWORD

The purpose of this book is (1) to give the general organization of the marching band; its relation to the concert band and to music education, and its value and place in the school and community; (2) to present the actual material to be used in instructing and developing the marching band in all necessary fundamentals and in the proper order; in so doing to furnish the drillmaster and drum major with definite directions as to the technic of drilling the band to obtain the best results; and (3) to make suggestions for the procedure to be followed in special formation and parade work.

The author wishes to acknowledge the helpful criticisms and the encouragement of many of his friends in the preparation of this book. He also desires to make known that the individual pictures included in the book were taken of outstanding students of the 1932 National Music Camp, Interlochen, Michigan, with the kind permission of Dr. Joseph E. Maddy. The pictures were taken immediately to the right of the famous Interlochen Bowl. The students are:

Drum major—Leslie Bruckshen, Elgin, Illinois.
The "bandsman"—Joe Rosensweig, Cleveland Heights, Ohio.
Trombone—Lyle Willis, Grand Rapids, Michigan.
Baritone—Eugene Davis, Chicago, Illinois.
Saxophone—Arthur Berg, Flint, Michigan.
French horn—James Reynolds, Flint, Michigan.
Field drum—Fred Fennell, Cleveland, Ohio.
Bass drum—William Ludwig, Jr., Elkhart, Indiana.
Piccolo—J. Henry Francis, Jr., Charleston, West Virginia.
Clarinet—Joe Rosensweig, Cleveland Heights, Ohio.
Cornet—Max Mitchell, Stillwater, Oklahoma.

Members of the Heights High School Band, Cleveland Heights, Ohio, posed for the pictures involving an entire band.

M. H.

TABLE OF CONTENTS

INTRODUCTION

(The following article, entitled "THE MARCHING BAND", is reprinted from the December, 1930 issue of the MUSIC SUPERVISORS JOURNAL).

IN spite of the rapidly changing fancies and the super-sophistication of the present day, people still crowd to the windows along the street or rise to their feet in the great stadia of this country at the sound of a marching band. Martial music and the rhythmic step of attractively uniformed musicians still have the power to inspire and stimulate, whatever the occasion. The band that can march well seldom lacks opportunities to display its ability along that line, and because of the tendency of human nature to be appealed to by the spectacular, more attention is brought to that band than ordinarily would be received.

The value of a good marching band to the school or institution to which it belongs and to the community can hardly be overestimated. It attracts the interest and affection of a large majority of the citizens who would permit the purely musical activities of the band to go unnoticed and unappreciated. It is an organization which everyone is proud to call "ours". It carries the name of its school or city with it wherever it goes and takes back popular recognition and acclaim from thousands of people. It is another project for which the community is glad to unite in support; it greatly aids in developing community spirit and progressiveness.

The value of the marching band to music education in general lies in its advertising power. It provides a strong incentive to all youth to study music so as to participate in band activities. Parents are quick to realize the worth of such an organization in a disciplinary way and as an outlet for some of the child's leisure time and surplus energy, and accept it also as providing an entrance to further musical culture, in which they are at the time probably more interested than the child himself.

In most communities at present there is a great amount of interest and importance attached to football games, and at those events the band performances are usually big attractions. It is here, perhaps, that the school band has the best opportunity to make itself popular. A popular organization of this kind inevitably draws part of its following to its concerts and thus performs a direct service to the cause of music education.

Granted that the school marching band serves a very useful purpose, there is still the question of its relation to the concert band, and the program of its training. With the ideal concert band consisting of about two-thirds reeds and woodwinds, and one-third brass and percussion, the volume and brilliance of its music on the march would not be as satisfactory as that of a band with a larger proportion of brass and percussion instruments; so for marching purposes it would be advisable whenever possible to augment those sections to approximately one-half the total number of players, from a second or reserve band. If this cannot be arranged, and a good "all-around" band is desired, perhaps it would be wise to maintain the brass and percussion sections in larger numbers than actually needed for concert work, using the extra players judiciously.

It must be realized of course that to develop a good marching band requires a great amount of time and effort. This undoubtedly is repaid and the band cannot but profit by it if the rest of its training is also properly managed. How then should the time allotted to the training of a band be proportioned as to marching and rehearsal?

I believe that every school band should know how to march, and be able to do credit to itself whenever occasion demands; I believe that the band that can play extremely well but marches very poorly is unbalanced, and that part of its legitimate education has been neglected.

There is no doubt that training in marching has certain educational value, and affects the bearing, self-control, and self-confidence of each band member in a very positive way. It is conducive to clear thinking and quick acting. However, we must not lose sight of the fact that the band is first of all a musical organization, and that a band is not a band until it can produce music. It just happens that marching and playing make a very happy combination, with results far more attractive than marching without music, or playing a military march without marching. The marching band is dependent upon the playing band for its very existence, never *vice versa*; a given group of musicians can be made into a marching band quite readily, barring physical defects, but it would take a long time to transform a group of soldiers into a playing band. Also, a good playing band may be developed without any knowledge of marching, and achieve much success in that field, but the best kind of a marching band is apt to go unnoticed unless its music is at least satisfactory.

Since, then, the *raison-d'etre* of a band is music, it seems reasonable that band training should be dominated by the musical idea, with the marching relegated to its proper place as quite an important element. The very first thing a band should do is to lay a foundation for future good playing. When it can play march music with some degree of proficiency it should learn to march. From then on the marching ability may be developed as rapidly as possible, so long as it does not seriously interfere with reasonable progress in playing.

It seems to be the customary practice in schools wherein instrumental music is highly developed to devote one period daily to band instruction, and this amount is considered adequate in the general educational scheme. If just this time or less is available, I would say that about one-fourth to one-fifth should be spent in marching practice during the outdoor season, which in the fall may be made to coincide with the football season, and in the spring may take up probably the last two months of the school term. In that time the fundamentals of marching may be taught to a degree which will do justice to the band's musical ability, and will add variety and interest to the general training program. However, if extra time is available outside of the regular rehearsal period, then it is fine to use it for drill purposes with a view to perfecting marching fundamentals and going beyond to prepare intricate maneuvers and formations for the entertainment of football crowds and parade spectators. There is no reason for limiting the amount of drill so long as it does not conflict with the regular rehearsals and jeopardize the musical instruction which is the primary object. In my school, physical education is required of all students three periods weekly, but band members are excused during the football season with the provision that that time is spent after school in band drill. This leaves the regular rehearsal period intact for musical training. Any arrangement of this kind is very satisfactory and worthwhile, and provides for the exceptional marching band without over-emphasizing that feature of it.

The school bandmaster should be prepared to instruct his band in marching as well as in playing. If there should be an expert drillmaster also on the faculty who is available for band service it might be well to enlist his aid for certain parts of the drill work, but the technic of the marching band is enough different from that of the usual marching group that the bandmaster should retain the general direction of it, and see that the marching and the music are perfectly correlated. The drum major should be a valuable assistant in all drill matters, and of course it is he who actually directs the marching of the band in performance. He should be able to carry on the drill work in the absence of the bandmaster, just as the student director is able to conduct a rehearsal when necessary, but it is hardly more practical to make the drum major entirely responsible for the correct marching of the band than to depend upon the student director for all of the musical training the band receives, for if band drill is worth doing at all it is worth doing well and with the proper supervision.

To further assist in the detail work of drilling there should be a "field" officer who does not play while marching, but who marches at the right of the front rank when in position, and does anything necessary to see that the drum major's commands and signals are carried out properly; in addition there should be officers of sections who act as officers of ranks on the field. These officers should be given special training so as to be able to assume charge of their ranks at any time. With this organization the bandmaster will be able to reach each member effectively, and will have a definite means of enforcing discipline, which is more of a problem on the drill field than in the rehearsal room.

Space will not permit going into detail in regard to the actual material for the instruction of the marching band. I can only mention briefly the things which I believe every good marching band should know and be able to carry out. * * * * * * * * * *

Any band which masters all the above movements will have enough of a marching repertoire to take care of it under almost any circumstances. The drum major must be a serious student of drilling maneuvers, must keep a cool head and know just what to do in any and all conditions. And any member of a band which is able to do all the above will affirm my statement that the marching band is a good training ground for clear thinking and decisive action.

As to special formations of letters and other symbols—they represent the originality and personality of each individual band, and an attempt to explain or standardize them would defeat the purpose of entertainment and surprise for which they are intended. However, the secret of success in all marching, whether regular or special, lies in getting everyone to do exactly the right thing at exactly the right time.

MARK H. HINDSLEY.

BAND—AT-TEN-TION!

Section I

FUNDAMENTALS OF THE MARCHING BAND

♪

A. Marching Formation

The basic marching formation of a band consists of rows of players extending from right to left called *ranks,* and rows extending from front to rear called *files.* The front rank is numbered "one" with the succeeding ones numbered in order. The files are numbered similarly from right to left. Each player is designated by the number of his file and the number of his rank; thus, the player in the fourth file and second rank is called "number 4 of rank 2". It is sometimes preferred to use the letters "A", "B", "C", etc., for the ranks, reserving the numbers for the files. In this case the player named above would have the designation "B4". If numbers are used for both ranks and files, each player's numbers may be combined, using the rank number first, such as "2-4" or "24".

There should be more ranks than files, making the band formation longer or "deeper" than wide. However, a "square" band is preferable to one more than twice as long as wide. It is always advisable to have an "even" number of files, *i.e.,* 4, 6, or 8, to facilitate many movements as may be seen later.

The spaces between the files are called the *interval,* and are equal to each other; the spaces between the ranks are also equal and are called the *distance.* The lengths of these spaces vary according to the conditions of marching. It is recommended, however, that in the fundamental marching formation both the interval and distance be taken as three 30 inch paces, or two and one-half yards, measuring from the center of one position to the center of the next. In parading on the football field, which is one of the chief functions of the school marching band, there will be two such spaces to each five-yard line. Thus the ranks and files may have an accurate check on their positions, one when marching the length of the field, the other when marching the width of the field,

For street parades the interval should approximate the above as nearly as possible for the most impressive appearance; however, it should never be greater than two and one-half yards, and many times it must be much less. Regardless of the interval, the distance should be constant throughout all stages of training and performance.

The marching formation is illustrated in Fig. 1.

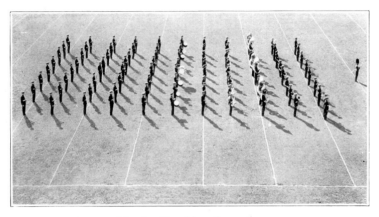

Fig. 1. Marching Formation

There are several different orders in which the instruments may be placed in ranks, with points of advantage in each. Both musical effect and appearance must be considered. It does not seem important or even wise to approximate the concert arrangement in the marching formation; at a reasonable distance almost all instruments have an equal chance of being heard in the best possible balance, and as the band "marches by" it is most impressive to hear the heavier toned instruments throughout, which may be accomplished by placing the brass both at the front and rear. The customary position of the trombones is in the front rank, because of their necessity for more than the regular distance to the front. Especially in large bands, the drums should be placed in a rank as near the center as possible, with the bass drum and cymbals in the center of the rank, to help "solidify" the band in marching and playing. For purposes of organization and appearance, "like" instruments should be placed in the same ranks where there are sufficient numbers, but of course "piecing" some ranks is almost always necessary.

For the reasons just given, the following order of instruments is recommended, from front to rear: trombones, baritones, horns, basses, saxophones, piccolos (flutes if used), drums, clarinets, trumpets, and cornets. Other instruments are seldom used on the march. If it is possible to choose the instrumentation desired, the following formation is suggested for a large marching band of eleven ranks and eight files:

First rank:	8 trombones
Second rank:	2 baritones, 6 horns
Third rank:	6 sousaphones, 2 baritones
Fourth rank:	8 saxophones
Fifth rank:	8 piccolos
Sixth rank:	6 field drums, 1 bass drum, 1 cymbal player
Seventh rank:	8 clarinets
Eighth rank:	8 clarinets
Ninth rank:	8 clarinets
Tenth rank:	6 trumpets, 2 cornets
Eleventh rank:	8 cornets

Larger or smaller bands may use instruments in these proportions, or assign in similar manner the instrumentation at hand. It is highly desirable to have a number of "reserves" in addition to the players in the regular formation, to fill in vacancies that may occur. Competition for regular positions will thus be keener, and will lead to greater efficiency. When all are present, the reserves may be placed in a rank within or at the end of the band, leaving "blank files" in their rank if necessary. They may be used in this manner in training or in street parades where no special formations are called for. When substituting in another rank, a reserve should carry an instrument which is proper in that place, whether he can play it or not.

Officers of sections should make up all of the first file in the marching formation; any remaining officers may be placed in the last file. Other players in each rank should be alternated according to their experience. Each rank may also be "dressed" or "balanced" according to the height of its members. Every position in the marching formation has its own responsibilities, but players showing the most initiative should be placed where it is felt their presence will have the greatest effect.

The director of the band should have mimeograph or blue print charts to facilitate making up the marching formation and for checking attendance. One similar to the form shown in Fig. 2 is recommended; names may be placed inside the blocks and on the lines in pencil, so as to be easily erased and changed.

_____BAND

Marching Formation

Date_____

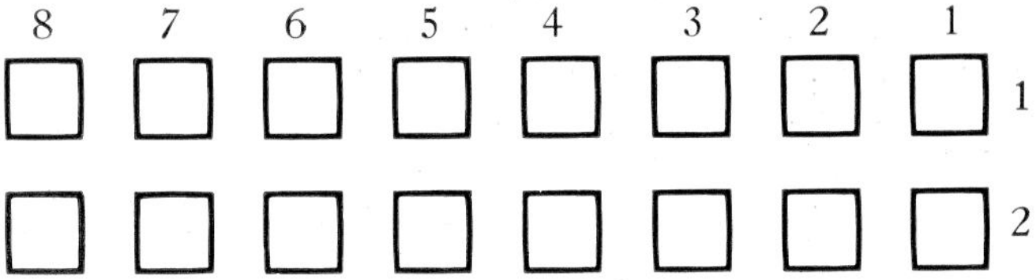

8	7	6	5	4	3	2	1	
□	□	□	□	□	□	□	□	1
□	□	□	□	□	□	□	□	2

etc.

Drum Major_____ Field Officer_____

Reserves

_____   _____   _____

_____   _____   _____

_____   _____   _____

Fig. 2

B.   OFFICERS AND COMMANDS

All marching maneuvers are executed upon *commands* or *signals* from the officer in charge. The director of the band usually acts as *drillmaster* also. At all appearances, however, the *drum major* acts as commanding officer, leading the band according to general or specific instructions previously given him by the director.   The drum major's regular position is five yards ahead of the center of the front rank. He may be given the title of *sergeant*.

The drum major must first of all possess executive ability of a high order, and be a person in whom the band members have confidence. Next, he must present a good appearance, and handle himself well in marching.   Third, he must understand the marching band, be able to give all the necessary commands and signals, and show his ability to maneuver the band deftly and quickly. If, in addition to these qualifications, he can twirl the baton with various manipulations, he will make a very successful drum major; the twirling, however, is not absolutely necessary, whereas the other characteristics are demanded.

Often a *field officer* may be appointed by the director to act as second in command to the drum major while the band is in marching formation. He should also have the title of *sergeant*. This officer does not play his instrument, but marches regularly immediately to the right of number one of the front rank, assisting the drum major and drillmaster whenever necessary, and possibly giving pistol signals for special formations. It is not advised that the drillmaster march with the band in performances that have been previously prepared, but it is recommended that he march with the band at other times, taking the place of the field officer, or marching in any other position he desires so that he can move about freely.

In addition to the drum major and field officer there should be other "non-commissioned" officers—*corporals* and *sergeants*—at least one for every eight bandsmen and not more than one for every five or six. They may be appointed by the director on the basis of musical and executive ability and class seniority. They should be divided among the various sections, so that there will be at least one officer in every marching rank, and not more than two. These officers should be able to assume charge of their ranks and give them proper instruction in frequent single rank drills. All officers should be given special advance training in marching and in their duties in connection with it, and may be allowed some freedom while the band is being trained in order to assist and instruct the players under them.

Most of the commands used by the average band may be given either verbally or by signal of the drum major's baton and whistle. There are some commands, however, which have no verbal counterpart, and others for which there are no signals. All of the movements should first be learned from the verbal commands if there are such, then the signals may be substituted. In performance the drum major *always* uses his baton and whistle for a command unless there is no signal for that command, or unless he wishes the drums to be silent during the execution of the command. In the latter case, the command should be given verbally, and the words "without the drums" prefaced to it. If the band should be marching without the drum beat, the commands may be given either verbally or by signal.

Most commands and signals have two parts—the *preparatory command* (or *signal*) and the *command* (or *signal*) of *execution*. A small interval of time should elapse between these two parts, and they should always be given as nearly as possible with the same time interval, so that the band can anticipate the final command or signal, which starts the movement.

The drum major's preparatory signal consists usually of twirling the baton around the right shoulder and bringing it to a certain position together with a long, loud blast of his whistle. The signal of execution is another movement of the baton with a short whistle. The methods described later in this book for giving these signals are perhaps more elaborate than former standard methods, but it has been found that they are more effective, both in precision and appearance. The actual positions of the baton which describe the movements to be executed are more or less the same as have always been used.

C. Conditions of Drill

A good place to drill is an obvious necessity to the marching band. It must be large enough to permit all manner of turns and maneuvers of the band being drilled. It should be level and free from all obstructions. The school football field usually is the most logical place to drill, if there is no conflict with the football team at the time of drill. If the band has to go a considerable distance to a field much valuable time will be wasted. Practice on the street is better than none at all, but very little besides straight marching and street parade work may be taught there. The best place to drill must be determined in each instance by local conditions, which vary considerably.

Every member of the band should be required to attend drill rehearsals, unless of course there is some unavoidable circumstance which prohibits. It should be made clear that marching is a part of the regular band training program, and anyone who takes band must take all of it. Every student will want to march when the band gains proficiency, but some few may seek to avoid it in the early stages of training. Irregular attendance cannot be tolerated in the good marching band, and heavy penalties should be meted out to any who are absent or tardy without a sufficient excuse. Each member should be made to feel his responsibility for a certain position, and to know that his absence either leaves a hole in the formation or requires a substitute, both of which are very much of a handicap to the work of the band.

Members of the band must report to drill with the proper equipment, which will include instrument, music lyre, march music, and any marching instructions issued. It is advantageous to supply all officers with small megaphones which they may hang about their necks with cords, to use in case of individual rank or section drill. The drum major should have his baton and a good whistle which may be attached to the clothing ready for instant use; the field officer should have a whistle and also pistols with blank cartridges if they are to be used for signals. The drillmaster should have a rather large but not unwieldy megaphone and a good whistle. It should be possible for him to drill the band occasionally from a permanent or temporary elevation, so that he may analyze its movements to better advantage. Every member should be instructed to wear clothing suitable to the weather, especially rubber protection for his feet in case the field is wet. Drill should not be held in the rain, but it will often be necessary to drill on a wet field. Drilling is very healthful exercise in spite of inclement weather and other adverse conditions, if each student will use good judgment in taking care of himself. If there are girls in the band, they should understand that low-heeled shoes are required for all marching. The property crew should see that the field is clear, and that any other equipment needed, such as yard signs, is in place.

Individual study and practice will greatly improve the results obtained by the band as a whole. The drum major and every other member can make good use of a mirror for observing and improving their positions and movements. Bad habits are easily formed and are hard to break, so every possible means should be employed to obtain accuracy from the start. Oral and written examinations are very valuable in the training schedule. Contests to determine the best drilled rank, officer, and "private", with suitable awards for each, also serve to increase enthusiasm and proficiency.

"Inspection" of the band by the drillmaster or other officers he designates should occur regularly, if possible, before each marching performance. Instruments should be in good playing condition, thoroughly cleaned and well polished; uniforms must be clean and well pressed and properly worn; insignia and decorations should appear in their proper positions; leather work and metal ornaments must be polished; all necessary equipment must be present and in place. A report of these things should be turned in to the band director and placed on the players' records.

Discipline on the drill field, both in rehearsal and performance, may be handled largely by the officers of the ranks through reports they are instructed to make on blanks provided for this purpose. Infractions of rules and regulations should materially affect the player's grade or standing in the band, and habitual offenders eventually should be eliminated.

The entire set-up of the marching band must show efficient organization. Proper attitude on the part of all players and officers must be developed so that no part of the work will be taken lightly. The drillmaster, drum major, and other officers must demand attention and precision, and give commands and instructions as though they expect them to be followed. The marching band is of necessity a military organization, and strict discipline tempered with good judgment will soon make an appeal to all affected by it. The instructor must retain a cool and dignified composure, and keep the band well in hand at all times. All orders and instruction should be short and to the point, and all movements repeated until they reach the desired perfection. Every opportunity should be taken to compliment individual band members, ranks, or the band in general; sarcasm and abuse will be of little avail. No personal feeling may be allowed to develop among the officers and any other players in any of the band's marching activities. Good judgment and tact on the part of the director in selecting the officers, and on the part of all officers in executing their duties, will make for complete harmony even with the strictness of the organization.

D.   THE TRAINING PROGRAM

Unit I

SCHOOL OF THE BANDSMAN

For the first exercises of the band, it is recommended that the players be placed in a single line abreast of each other; if one line would be too long, two lines may be formed ten yards apart and facing each other. Officers may be evenly spaced a few yards behind the lines, each one assigned to observe a certain group of players immediately ahead. The drillmaster and drum major may station themselves at the end of or between the lines, where all may see and hear. Only the experienced drummers or some especially trained for this particular stage of drilling should have their instruments; other band members will not need their instruments or music for the first few rehearsals.

EXERCISE 1.   ATTENTION
Command: "Band—At-ten—TION (shun)!"

(The preparatory commands will be written in small letters, and the commands of execution in capitals).

Fig. 3
The Position of ATTENTION

Exactly with the command of execution each player brings himself to the *position of attention,* which may be described as follows:

Heels together, feet turned out equally, forming an angle of about 45 degrees; knees straight but not stiff; body erect with weight distributed evenly; chest high, shoulders square and well back; chin in, head and eyes straight to the front; arms and hands hanging naturally at the sides, thumb and fingers extended and joined; body alert but not tense; no moving or talking.

At the preparatory command the heels should be slightly separated, so that the execution of the command will bring about a simultaneous click of the heels and snap into position in which all members take part. The carriage and appearance of the body will be improved if in addition to the above directions the hips are drawn back a trifle, eliminating the tendency of leaning backwards. The rule regarding no moving, no talking, or even smiling should be distinctly understood and carried out. It is very impressive to see the band stand absolutely immobile at attention, before or immediately after any maneuver. It adds much to the band's dignity and attitude. *The band must be at attention before any subsequent command may be given,* except in one instance which is explained in Exercise 3.

This exercise and subsequent exercises should first be taught from the verbal command, then with the drum major's signals. For the preparatory signal the drum major grasps the baton near the *ball* with the right hand, little finger next to the ball, places the *ferrule* of the baton on the ground against the right foot, right arm extended to the side, left hand on the hip, arm and hand preferably

straight at the wrist, fingers pointing forward and the thumb to
the rear—all as in Fig. 4, and blows a long blast on his whistle;
then he snaps the baton under his right arm with a short whistle
to complete the signal, leaving the baton in that position, which is
shown in Fig. 5. In both the command and signal a reasonable
amount of time must be allowed between the preparatory element
and the execution, to make sure everyone is ready to come to attention; both must be given in a bold and commanding way to indicate
business is meant. *No movement* should be allowed after the final
signal, even though someone is out of position; he will soon learn
to get in position before the signal of execution. The drum major
may face toward or away from the band in giving this signal,
depending upon what is to follow.

Fig. 4   Fig. 5
"Band—At-ten—   —TION!"

The drum major brings himself to the position of attention before giving any signal. His left hand remains on the hip, as
described, all the time he is at attention, unless he needs it for a
baton signal or for manipulation of his whistle. The position shown

in Fig. 5 is also the position in which he carries the baton "on the march" when the band is not playing or when he is not giving signals.

EXERCISE 2.   AT EASE
Command: "AT EASE!"

Fig. 6
The Position of AT EASE

This command needs no preparation. For band purposes, each player sets his left foot about 12 inches from the right and on the same line, and joins his hands at the back as illustrated in Fig. 6. This is a position of relaxation, *but there must be no talking or other disturbance.* The drillmaster or drum major may often wish to give further instructions during this time, and there must be no interruption.

The drum major's signal for this movement is simply to drop the baton to the ground with a short whistle, to the same position as shown in Fig. 4. The band must understand that after they are called to attention they are *always* at attention unless the drum major's baton is on the ground, or unless no subsequent command or signal has been given

since *At Ease* or *Rest,* which will be explained in the next exercise.

EXERCISE 3.   REST
Command: "REST!"

The only requirement in the execution of this command is that the right foot be kept in the player's position on the "line of march". Talking and any reasonable body position is allowed; this is the *only* occasion in marching formation when silence need not be maintained. Playing an instrument on the drill field should be against regulations, unless the band as a whole is playing under proper direction.

There is no signal for this command. *Rest* may be given with the band either at *Attention* or *At Ease*. The allied commands *Fall Out* and *Dismissed* should be given from *Attention;* the first implies that the band break ranks, but remain close at hand, ready for the commands *Fall In* and *Attention;* the second gives the band permission to disperse.

EXERCISE 4. RIGHT DRESS
Command: "Right—DRESS!"

Fig. 7
The Position of RIGHT DRESS

At this command all players except the one on the extreme right of each line turn their heads sharply to the right and align themselves properly by glancing down the line, and moving up or back until it is possible to see only the "line of eyes"; at the same time each player except the one on the extreme left of each line places the left hand on the left hip, thumb and fingers down, elbow extended straight to the left, and adjusts his position so that his right arm just touches the elbow of the player to his right. No one should lean forward or backward to correct the alignment, but must remain erect. This placement must be made quickly and accurately, for when anyone moves every one in the line to his left must move also; any one who cannot find his place will cause confusion and destroy the possibility of a straight line.

At the command *"FRONT!"* each player resumes the original position of attention, looking straight to the front. The interval between the members of the band will now be uniform, and sufficient for executing movements without the instruments. This interval will be assumed in "close formation", which will be referred to later. When the band is in formation with the regular interval, *Right Dress* will be executed without using the left arm and without closing to the right.

There are no drum major's signals for the commands *Right Dress* and *Front*.

EXERCISE 5. RIGHT FACE
Command: "Right—FACE!"

This movement is completed in two counts in marching cadence after the command of execution. On the first the body is turned 90 degrees to the right, pivoting on the right heel and left toe, keeping the legs straight; on the second count the left foot is brought up even with the right in the position of attention. The position of the feet on the first count is shown in Fig. 8. The facings should all be practiced slowly at first, until the pivot points are well established, then they may be done up to tempo. If in practice the band members will supply aloud the counts "*One! two!*" after the command, it will induce rhythmic precision.

There are no baton signals for the facings.

Fig. 8
RIGHT FACE—Count One

EXERCISE 6. LEFT FACE
Command: "Left—FACE!"

The facing to the left is executed similarly to *Right Face*, except that the body is turned 90 degrees to the left on the left heel and right toe, and the right foot is brought up to the left.

EXERCISE 7. ABOUT FACE
Command: "About—FACE!"

Two counts are used for this movement also. On the first count the right toe is placed slightly back of and to the left of the left heel, and on the second

Fig. 9
ABOUT FACE—Count One

the body is turned to the right to the reverse direction, ending with the feet in the correct position for attention.

A little slow practice will enable the player to find the right place for his right toe, and if he is careful to turn on the left *heel* instead of the left *toe,* he will soon find the turn comparatively easy to do correctly. It will be observed that the body does the entire turn on the *second* count, none of it on the first, as in the two preceding exercises; also that the turn is made by applying weight and pressure to the right toe, and not by the momentum of a swing from the body.

All the facings must be executed with precise, military movements, keeping the body strictly in the position of attention, as far as possible, throughout. All movement must begin on "one" and end on "two", with a distinctly separate movement for each count, not running the two movements together.

The commands for the facings may be given only when the band is standing at attention and not playing.

EXERCISE 8.   MARK TIME
Command: "Mark time—MARCH!"

Marching tempo or cadence in military regulations is 128 beats to the minute. Beginning with the left foot on the next beat in this tempo after the command *"Mark time—MARCH!",* the feet are raised 3 to 4 inches from the ground and replaced alternately on each succeeding beat without moving the body from position. This should be done briskly, bending the knees and swinging the arms naturally but energetically. The hips should be kept as nearly as possible on their original level. For the present the cadence should be kept by the drillmaster or other officer calling sharply *"One! two! one! two!"* or *"Left! right! left! right!"* It should be seen that the player's foot strikes the ground *exactly* on the beat, not anticipating it or lagging behind; it must also be seen that he starts with the correct foot—the *left*—and remains "in step".

There is no baton signal for this command. Exercise 8 should be studied and illustrated with Exercise 9 before it is used.

EXERCISE 9. THE HALT
Command: "Band—HALT!"

After the command *"HALT!"* one more step is taken (in position when marking time), and on the second count the other foot is brought in place beside the first, each player remaining *motionless* until a subsequent command is given. Precision in executing this command may be developed by thinking of it as *"HALT! one! two!"*, with all movement ending on *"two"*. Uniformity may

Fig. 10	Fig. 11
"Band—	—HALT!"

be secured by always giving the command of execution on the *left* foot, although actually it may be given on either. In bringing the last foot in place a good effect may be produced by swinging it slightly to the side and snapping it into position with a click of the heels; this must not be exaggerated, however.

The drum major's signals for the halt are illustrated in Figs. 10 and 11. The preparatory signal consists of "twirling" the baton around the right shoulder three or four times, facing the band (if not already in that position), raising the baton to arm's length above the head and letting the ferrule fall to the left hand in a horizontal position, with a long blast of the whistle beginning and ending with the twirl; for the signal of execution the baton is brought down to the level of the hips, close to the body, with a short whistle. The drum major may also bring the baton to shoulder level on the *"one"* and down again on *"two"*, with short whistles on each count, to aid in the precision of the halt.

Fig. 12
Starting Position for the Twirl

The "twirl" used in almost all preparatory signals is accomplished by bringing the baton back, across, and above the right elbow, then starting the twirl forward by a motion of the wrist, keeping the baton outside the right arm, which remains almost motionless, with the upper arm against the body. Three or four times around at moderate speed, with the whistle blowing constantly during the twirl, is usually sufficient to call the attention of the band to the signal. The starting position for the twirl is shown in Fig. 12.

When the band can execute the *Mark Time* and *Halt* cleanly and precisely by using the counts, with both the verbal commands and the signal, the drums may be brought into use. For marking time and marching, the drums play a four-measure repeating figure, based on the following rhythm:

Fig. 13

Variations of this figure are used by different bands to provide a more interesting one—for more variety and less monotony. An example of one actually used is given in Fig. 14.

Fig. 14

(L and R signify "left" and "right" sticks to be used by field drummers).

The drums start this figure on the first beat after the command *"MARCH!"*, and play it over and over. A fact of prime importance to drummers is that *no figure used in marching is ever broken into or interrupted by subsequent signals of the drum major*—they are always finished in their entirety before any different beat is begun, or before discontinued.

When the drum major gives the preparatory signal to halt, the drums finish the marching figure they are then playing, and follow it immediately with a special four-measure "halt figure". On the first beat of the third measure of this figure the drum major gives the signal of execution, with the subsequent raising and lowering of the baton on *"one"* and *"two"* as mentioned before.

Following is the drum beat for the halt, showing the proper place for the signal of execution, and its equivalent in the verbal command:

Fig. 15

The drummers stop playing as soon as the halt figure is completed. The drum major should time his preparatory signal so that the baton is raised near the middle of a marching figure, leaving no doubt in the mind of the first drummer as to when to start the halt figure. The remaining field drummers substitute the first measure of the marching figure for the first measure of the halt figure, thus taking their "cue" from the first drummer.

By making use of the drums in the halt, as just described, much greater precision and consistency will be possible than by the usual method of the drum major's signal alone.

From now on the drums should play for every marching movement of the band—for every step the band takes—unless "without the drums" is specified with the command, or unless the drum major gives the signal *"Cease Beat!"* This permits marching quietly, or with the cadence of the drums or music of another band. The position of the baton for the signal *"Cease Beat!"* is shown in Fig. 16. The drum major twirls the baton with the long whistle, faces the band, marching backward, and brings the baton to a vertical position pointing down, with the ball of the baton extending upward at arm's length, and the ferrule grasped by the left hand. The drums cease playing as soon as they have completed the marching figure just started, then the drum major returns the baton to the carry position and resumes the forward march. To begin the drum figure while marching, the drum major again faces the band, marching backward, and gives the verbal command *"Resume the beat—MARCH!"* The command of execution is given on the right foot, and the drums begin playing on the next beat.

Fig. 16
"CEASE BEAT!"

Fig. 17
"DRUMS ON THE SHELL!"

At other times it may be advantageous to have only the field drums furnish the cadence, and that on the shells of the drums instead of the heads. If they will do this strongly enough everyone in the band can hear it and march to it. At the same time it will be possible for officers to give verbal commands, instructions, and corrections while the band is marching. It is practical to use this method for the cadence also to avoid disturbing another event which is in progress in the same place or nearby, for instance, in marching on the football field during a preliminary game, and proceeding to the band members' seats. The drum major's signal for this kind of drum beat is given in the same manner as the signal for *Cease Beat,* with the position of the baton reversed—ball down—as in Fig. 17. Commands may be given either verbally or by signal while the drummers are playing on the shells, depending upon which seems the most appropriate. It is not wise for the drum major to use his whistle for signals while a game is in progress, as it may easily be confused with the referee's whistle. The regular drum beat may be resumed by the verbal command as explained before.

Perhaps there will be no need for the signals *Cease Beat* and *Drums on the Shell* in the training of the band thus far, but the drillmaster, drum major, and the drum section should be aware of the possibilities of their use later on.

Following the drillmaster's general instruction of the first nine exercises to the entire group assembled, it is advisable to have each officer assume charge of the group of players assigned to him for this drill period, for further specific instruction and assistance. If plans have been carefully made and carried out, it will be possible to cover all this training material, in both the large and small groups, in an one-hour drill period. The next drill period may be devoted to further perfecting these exercises, or to new material. The drillmaster should take occasion to review the preliminary exercises almost every time the band forms for drill; their repetition will increase precision, and also will help to develop the proper military attitude for the more difficult exercises.

The Training Program

Unit II

MARCH AND COUNTERMARCH

The band now may be formed in the regular marching formation, and all the conditions and terms of that formation fully explained to the members. Each player should have a definite place in the formation, so that at the command or signal *"Fall In!"* the band may form quickly and without confusion. The drum major takes his place *facing* the desired location of the band and gives the preparatory signal for *Attention.* This signal also implies the position and attitude *At Ease,* and each player goes to his place *silently* and awaits the next signal. Number one of the front rank takes his place first, since the entire band gets its position from him; the drum major may thoughtfully indicate to this player his position before giving the signal *"Fall In!";* soon he will be able to gauge his location accurately and entirely from that of the drum major. The other members of the first rank and first file must find their places immediately afterward to establish "guides" for the remaining players.

When all are in place the drum major brings the band to attention. The first rank should be made responsible for establishing the correct interval, and the first file the correct distance. This may be checked by the drum major and field officer. Each player back of the front rank must "cover down in file", getting *directly* behind the player in front of him so he can scarcely see anyone else in the file; when the command *Right Dress* is given it will be necessary for him to move only forward or backward for correct alignment. The drum major should check the alignment of the files, and the officers on the right of each rank the alignment of their ranks, with the field officer assisting wherever necessary. Members of the second rank must realize that they control the direction of their files, and the members of the second file must know they are responsible for the direction of their ranks; they must exercise great care in placing themselves properly so that the correct interval and distance will be maintained throughout the band. When the band is thoroughly accustomed to marching, it should not often be necessary to give the command *Right Dress* or to check alignment before the band begins to march, for everyone will be able to "fall in" at the proper place, and the command *Attention* will bring the entire band into accurate formation.

The first nine exercises may now be repeated in the new formation. Each player should be conscious all the time of maintaining straight ranks, straight files, and even straight diagonals, while executing these various movements in position. Nothing less than the very best efforts toward perfection should be accepted by any member of the organization. The manner in which these first fundamental movements are worked out will indicate the success of the band in the next stages of training.

Many of the next exercises may be taught more advantageously with the ranks in "close formation" but with the proper distance. They will then be easier to do in the regular open formation.

EXERCISE 10. FORWARD MARCH
Command: "Forward—MARCH!"

When the preparatory command *"Forward"* is given, the weight of the body should be shifted to the right foot, imperceptibly, and on the first beat after the command *"MARCH!"* each player steps forward on the left foot with a *full* step and continues to march. The drums play the repeating figure as given in the exercise on marking time.

The regulation step is 30 inches long; however, for school bands any step of 24 to 30 inches is satisfactory, depending upon the age and size of the members, and upon whether or not a faster tempo than 128 is desired. For football and "pep" parades the cadence is often between 136 and 144, and the step should be correspondingly shorter; for these parades it has been found that seven steps to each five yards is very practical. It is advisable to teach the band the length of step determined upon by using the yard marks or others similar.

For ordinary parade work the cadence should remain very constant at 128, and the step should be of a length easily taken by all members. The drum major is directly responsible for the pace of the band, with number one of the front rank maintaining at all times the proper distance behind the drum major; together they should avoid a jerky pace caused by shortening or lengthening the step; the band must always give the impression of "getting somewhere". The players in the center of the front rank must always keep their relative positions behind the drum major, with those on each side taking the proper interval from the center.

Bands differ greatly in their manner of marching; as in nearly everything else the results obtained depend upon the effort put into it. Good marching requires effort—not so much physical as mental; the whole spirit and possibility of achievement of the marching band may be seen by watching it march straight down the field, without any maneuvers on the way. Band members must catch the rhythm and spirit of the march quickly and enthusiastically, then it inevitably will be caught by the spectators.

The step in marching should be snappy, with each player seeming to be "playing the drums with his heels"; the body should be carried easily and naturally in the position of attention without being jolted by the impact of the feet, with the arms swinging and the knees bending as described in marking time—not with the feet dragging along close to the ground as some do in ordinary walking. It will require only a little mental effort for each player to look and feel his height and importance and to take a real pride in his marching. "Guide" is always to the right unless otherwise specified; each player must glance in that direction out of the "corner of his eye", while covering down in file and maintaining correct interval and distance. *No one can be permitted to forget for one instant to check on his position,* for the positions of many others and the appearance of the entire band depend to a great extent on each member. It must be seen also that the entire band keeps *in step.*

Fig. 18
"Forward——"

The drum major's preparatory signal for the *Forward March* consists of the twirl of the baton with a long whistle (facing away from the band), and bringing the baton to a position pointing diagonally forward and up from the right shoulder at arm's length, as in Fig. 18. For the signal of execution the drum major brings the ball of the baton back to the right shoulder and immediately jabs it back to arm's length with a short whistle. He may leave it in that position for the first step, then let the ferrule end fall, with the baton doing another complete turn about the shoulder before falling into position under the arm on the fourth step. The drum major must be sure to step off correctly on his own signal.

The drum major may give the signal for the halt with the drum figure as described in Exercise 9, marching backward at a *full* step until it is executed. The band may then *About Face* and march in the reverse direction, remembering always to *guide right*. A precise forward march with a full step on the first beat and a clean halt should be developed. The band should become somewhat accustomed to marching before attempting the succeeding exercises.

The "half step" is used in many marching maneuvers. If seven full steps are taken for each five yards, then fourteen half steps will be needed to cover the same distance. The band may be taught to march together at the half step, with the verbal command *"Half step—MARCH!"* either at the halt or while the band is marching; full step is resumed by the command or signal for *Forward March*. Both the full step and the half step must be accurate if the maneuvers in which they are used are to be accurate.

EXERCISE 11. THE COUNTERMARCH

Command: "To the Rear (or 'Countermarch')—MARCH!"

When the command *"To the Rear"* is given in the army each man turns individually and begins to march immediately in the reverse direction; however, it is understood that at this command the band marching with the troops does a "countermarch", in order to remain in the same position from front to rear. Either *"To the Rear"* or *"Countermarch"* may be used as a preparatory command in drilling the band, although usually it will be taken care of by the drum major's signal.

For the countermarch signal the drum major twirls the baton with a long whistle, faces the band, brings the baton up to position as in *Forward March,* and *marks time*; when the front rank comes abreast of him he gives the signal *"MARCH!"* in the new direction, and marches between the center files of the band, twirling the baton slowly or bringing it under his arm. The countermarch signal is usually given while the band is marching, although it may be given from the halt in a similar manner. The drum major gives the signal on the line where he desires the turn to be made.

The standard and simplest method of countermarching consists of having the front rank players in the right half of the band turn immediately about to the right, and those on the left turn about to the left, and all march back alongside and outside their files; each succeeding rank executes the same movement as it reaches the line on which the front rank turned. As each rank clears the rear of the band it shifts to right and left to reestablish the proper interval between the center files. This type of countermarch is illustrated in Fig. 19. The disadvantage of this method is that it places the band in reverse formation as to right and left, which is apt to confuse the players in other maneuvers, and will lead to difficulties in special formations. However, it is a very direct method, and may be executed with the entire band either at full step or half step, as desired. The band must be in "open" formation for the *Countermarch*.

Fig. 19
THE COUNTERMARCH (1)

Several other methods for the *Countermarch* may be devised with the band emerging in regular formation. The movement recommended here is shown in Fig. 20.

At the signal the right half of the front rank executes an arc to the left, and the left half an arc to the right inside the first arc, and the entire rank marches back in a straight line through the remainder of the band. The halves of the rank meet telescopically when each has half completed its 180 degree arc. The players in the outside files march at a *full step* during the turn, with the "pivots" moving very slowly, governing their steps to remain in the line of the arcs. When the entire rank is turned it marches in the new direction at a *half step*. The remaining ranks of the band march at a *half step* at the signal; as each rank reaches the line established by the front rank when the countermarch began, it executes the arcs in the same manner as prescribed for the front rank. During the actual turns of each rank *guide* is in *both direc-tions;* after the turns guide again becomes *right.* As each rank clears the rear of the band it shifts to the left one-half an interval, to continue down the original file paths.

When the drum major clears the rear rank of the band he should turn about to the right and march backward with very short steps; when the front rank reaches the proper distance from him, he in-creases his step to a half step; if it becomes necessary for him to regulate the alignment or to further check the pace, he may bring the baton to a horizontal position at shoulder level; when the en-tire band is marching in the new direction, the drum major turns about and gives the signal for *Forward March,* with the band re-suming the full step at once. This last signal may be eliminated if the band is trained to begin marching at a full step simultaneoulsy as soon as the drum major turns about.

Fig. 20
THE COUNTERMARCH (2)

This countermarch movement may be developed accurately by having each rank go through the movement alone, then the right half of the band together, then the left half together. With the *Forward March* and *Countermarch* exercises the band will be able to march up the field and back again without stops, and thus can get in some telling marching practice.

THE TRAINING PROGRAM
Unit III
POSITIONS OF INSTRUMENTS

So far no one has carried his instrument on the field except the
experienced drummers, for it has been desired to teach the first
movements without unnecessary encumbrances. From this time on
the rule should be made that everyone report to drill with his instrument, music lyre, and music, unless otherwise specified; each
player will need to become accustomed to the conditions of carrying his instrument while marching, even though no playing may
be done for some time.

For the sake of uniformly good appearance there are two specific
positions for the instruments in the marching formation—the
carry position ("*at the carry*"), and the *playing position*. The playing positions are the same as in concert formation, and need not be
discussed here; the *carry* positions parallel the *rest* positions in
concert formation.

Fig. 21   Fig. 22
Trombone   Baritone, Upright Tuba

The carry positions are designed to take advantage of all vertical and horizontal military lines wherever possible, and arranged to make it possible to bring them to the playing positions with the simplest and quickest single movement. Figs. 21 to 29 illustrate these positions.

Trombone: Held vertically in front of the center of the body with the left hand in playing position, left forearm horizontal, right arm free; slide tubings equidistant from body. The instrument may be tilted slightly backward while marching, if it interferes with the knees, or else held in a diagonal position across the body; the latter method, however, destroys the desired vertical military line.

Baritone, Upright Tuba: "Top action" baritones and tubas are held by the left hand at the playing angle, slightly lowered or tilted from the mouth, right arm free; the tuba should be supported also by a strap around the shoulder. "Side action" instruments are held in similar manner by the right hand, with the left arm free.

Fig. 23
French Horn

Fig. 24
Saxophone

Horns: The French horn is held in front of the body, left fore-arm horizontal, right hand in bell. The mellophone is held similarly, with the right forearm horizontal, and the left hand on the bell. Perhaps their appearance would be better if the French horn were held under the right arm and the mellophone under the left, bells back, leaving one arm free; however, more than one movement would then be required to bring the instruments to their playing positions, so the latter positions are not recommended.

Sousaphone, or *Helicon Bass*: Balanced on the shoulder with the left hand, right arm free at the side.

Saxophone (curved): Supported at the side by a strap, right hand in playing position on the instrument, which is tilted slightly forward; left arm free. The same directions apply also to *alto clarinet, bass clarinet*, and *bassoon*. The straight model saxophone is carried like the Bb clarinet.

Field Drum: Field and snare drums are supported by a strap over the right shoulder, resting at the playing angle against the left leg between the knee and hip; the sticks are held by the right

Fig. 25
Field Drum

Fig. 26
Bass Drum

hand in a horizontal position straight forward under the right arm, left arm free.

Bass Drum: Supported by a strap around the shoulders, and held in front of and against the body at a comfortable height, in an exactly vertical position; the bass drum stick is held in the same manner as the snare drum sticks. It is not advised that one or more persons assist the bass drummer in carrying his instrument; it makes a very unwieldy arrangement in the marching formation. One man is able to carry a large enough bass drum to provide ample volume for most bands.

Cymbals: Held at the sides at arm's length, one in each hand, vertically.

The cymbal player must memorize the music to be played on the march. The bass drummer may easily use a music lyre attached to his instrument. The field drummers must either memorize their music accurately or use the lyre attachment; the former is to be preferred.

Fig. 27
Piccolo

Fig. 28
Clarinet

Piccolo and *Flute*: Held vertically in front of the center of the body with the right hand, right forearm horizontal, left arm free.

Fig. 29
Cornet

Clarinet: Held vertically in front of the center of the body with the right hand in playing position, right forearm horizontal, left arm free. The music lyre should be placed in the middle of the clarinet, not at the bottom, to avoid looking down when marching. The *oboe* is held in the same manner as the clarinet.

Cornet and *Trumpet*: Held vertically in front of the center of the body with the left hand; fingers around the valves as in playing position, thumb withdrawn slightly; valve tips pointing straight ahead; left forearm horizontal, right arm free.

The instruments are to be carried carefully in these positions whenever the band is at attention and not playing. The free arm, if any, is to continue to swing while marching. When the player is *At Ease*, the instrument may be held in any comfortable way, with the free hand at the back, but it must be brought to the carry position with a "snap" as the heels click at the command *Attention*, and held absolutely still.

All the drums may now be used for the marching figures. When a preparatory command or signal indicates the marching figure is to be played in a movement, the drummers quickly and quietly bring their sticks to a poised position above their drums, ready to play immediately after the command or signal of execution.

THE TRAINING PROGRAM
Unit IV
THE TURNS

Many sets of directions for turning the band to the right or left may be drawn up; however, most of them are based on two main types which we may call the *wheel* turn and the *oblique* turn. Turns of the former type involve "wheeling" the band about on a "fixed pivot" or set of pivots; in the latter type "moving pivots" are used, with the rest of the band arriving in position by one or two "oblique" movements.

The advantage of the wheel turn over the oblique turn is that it maintains a "solid", or straight front rank throughout, as against a "broken" front during the turn. It is a much slower and tedious turn, however, if the band is large and the pivot is absolutely "fixed". A variation of the wheel turn in which the pivot does move slightly, but not enough to disrupt the solidity of each rank, is thought to be the most practical turn of this type; it will be the only one illustrated here, along with the oblique type of turn.

EXERCISE 12.   COLUMN RIGHT
Command: "Column Right—MARCH!"

This movement is used for the band to turn a square corner, 90 degrees to the right. At the command or signal of execution the front rank takes *one more step forward,* then executes an arc 90 degrees to the right, with the pivot moving *immediately* in the new direction at a *quarter step,* and the left flank man marching at a *full step; guide* is in *both directions* during the arc, with the interval taken from the moving pivot, which causes the arc to deflect slightly to the right. When the entire rank is turned in the new direction it proceeds at a *half step.* The remainder of the band slows to the half step at the signal for the turn; as each rank reaches the line on which the front rank started the turn it follows the same directions as prescribed for the front rank. The pivot men will retain the regular distance from the rank in front until they have turned in the new direction, when it will immediately be decreased to half the regular distance; however, as each rank completes the turn and moves forward, the correct distance will again be obtained. When the entire band is turned it moves forward at a full step with the drum major.

The movement just described is based on the *wheel* turn. It is illustrated in Fig. 30.

Fig. 30
The COLUMN RIGHT (1)

The *Column Right* in the *oblique* style of turn is shown in Fig. 31. At the command or signal of execution the front rank takes *one more step forward;* the pivot turns *immediately* in the new direction and marches forward at a *half step;* at the same time every other player in the front rank turns 45 degrees to the right, and marches "obliquely" in that direction at a *full step, keeping the rank straight;* as each player reaches a point directly ahead of the original first file of the band, he again turns 45 degrees to the right and marches at a full step until he comes abreast of the rest of his rank, then proceeds at a *half step.*

If a very quick turn is desired, the remaining ranks of the band may move up to the point of turn at a full step, each rank turning in exactly the same manner and on the same ground as the front rank; as the last man in each rank comes abreast of his rank, the entire rank marches forward at a full step. This method, however, will close almost all of every rank to half the regular distance for a short period of time before the turn is completed, and is objectionable from that standpoint. It is recommended that all ranks back of the front rank march at the *half step after the signal,* until they reach the line on which the turn began, and that the front rank be held to the *half step* by the drum major until the entire band is marching in the new direction. In this way the pivots of all ranks will keep their regular distance from the man in front at all times during the turn; it will take a little more time to complete the turn, but will be less confusing.

Fig. 31
The COLUMN RIGHT (2)

In either of the turns described, each player must march *straight up the file paths* to the line on which the front rank started the turn, avoiding the tendency to swing to the left. The pivot men must be very accurate with their quarter, half, and full steps; the ranks must guide properly, and await the turn of their pivots before beginning their wheel or oblique movements.

To develop the type of turn chosen it is advisable to conduct intensive single rank drills, and drills with the pivot men alone. The individual ranks may count the number of steps or half steps required for them to reach the line of turn, and practice their movement as it is actually done in the complete formation. Drill for a few minutes in closed formation will help to establish the correct ideas in the minds of the band members, before attempting the exercise in the regular open formation.

Fig. 32
"Column Right—"

The drum major's preparatory signal for the _Column Right_ consists of the twirl of the baton with the long whistle, bringing it to arm's length pointing straight up from the right shoulder, then _immediately_ down to the right to a horizontal position at arm's length, as shown in Fig. 32; the drum major turns his head to the right as the baton reaches that position, and glances back over his shoulder to watch the position of the front rank. One step before the front rank reaches the point desired for the turn—on the _right foot,_ if possible, he pulls the ball of the baton to his shoulder and immediately jabs it back to the right with a short whistle, for the signal of execution. If the wheel turn is used, he then turns about to the right and faces the band, with the baton held horizontally in both hands at shoulder level, marching backward through an arc to the new direction, regulating the pace and alignment of the front rank. When the entire band has turned he faces front and gives the signal _Forward March,_ unless the band has been informed that his turning to the front is sufficient signal in itself for the full step. If the oblique type of turn is used, he needs not face the band until he has completed the two oblique movements at a full step to his own position; after he has done this the procedure is the same as described above.

EXERCISE 13. COLUMN LEFT

Command: "Column Left—MARCH!"

Fig. 33
"Column Left—"

At this command the band executes a turn 90 degrees to the left, following the same general directions as given for *Column Right,* only in the reverse direction. The drum major gives his signal in the same way, except that he brings the baton down to the left to a horizontal position, as in Fig. 33, turns his head to the left, gives the signal on the *left foot* if possible, and, in the wheel turn, turns about to the left to face the band.

EXERCISE 14. COLUMN HALF RIGHT

Command: "Column Half Right —MARCH!"

This turn is only 45 degrees to the right, otherwise it is very similar to the *Column Right.* If the oblique turn is used, the players will need execute only one right oblique movement individually, marching immediately in the new direction. For the drum major's preparatory signal the baton is brought to a horizontal position, 45 degrees to the right, as in Fig. 34, after the preliminary twirl and movement described in the signal for *Column Right.*

EXERCISE 15. COLUMN HALF LEFT

Command: "Column Half Left—MARCH!"

The *half left turn* is 45 degrees to the left, and is done similarly to the *Column Left.* The baton points horizontally in this direction, as shown in Fig. 35, for the preparatory signal.

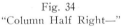

Fig. 34   Fig. 35
"Column Half Right—"   "Column Half Left—"

Pointing the baton straight up at arm's length at the end of the twirl, and bringing it immediately down to a horizontal position at arm's length, are characteristic of the signals for the turns; all of the signals for the four turns should be given in the same general way, except as to the final direction of the baton. Those in the back of the band may quite readily understand signals given in this way, even though they may not see the final position of the baton.

THE TRAINING PROGRAM

Unit V

PLAYING IN MARCHING FORMATION

EXERCISE 16. RAISING THE INSTRUMENTS

Command: "Instruments—UP!"

When the band is in marching formation it is very desirable for all instruments to be raised simultaneously in preparation for playing, and with precise, military movements. The verbal command as given above is very seldom used, except in explaining the drum major's signal. After the usual twirl and long whistle, the baton is brought to the right shoulder, pointing up and slightly to the right; then with a short whistle it is pushed in that direction to arm's length for the signal of execution. These baton positions are illustrated in Figs. 36 and 37.

Fig. 36   Fig. 37
"Instruments—   —UP!"

The instruments are raised to their playing positions with a single "flash", as nearly as possible *simultaneously* with the signal of execution, and remain motionless. Everything should be adjusted perfectly so that *no extra movement* of the instrument or of any part of the body is necessary immediately before or after the signal. The free hand is brought to its place on the instrument at the same time the instrument is raised; only the hand which is originally on the instrument should be used for raising it. The instruments should be played in their correct standard positions, taking advantage of all natural horizontal and diagonal lines, with the head squarely on the shoulders and straight to the front. The trombones, cornets, and trumpets are especially noticeable, and must be held *exactly horizontally* for the best appearance of the band. Field drummers should use their sticks uniformly, and raise them well up at every opportunity, while playing.

For lowering the instruments, to complete the exercise, the drum major brings the baton down across the body, with a short whistle; the instruments are lowered to their carry positions on the next beat.

EXERCISE 17. STARTING TO PLAY AT THE HALT

The preparatory signal for starting to play is the *raise of instruments*. The drum major acts as musical director when the band is in marching formation. After the instruments are raised he indicates the start of the piece by jerking the baton slightly to the left with a short whistle, as an "up-beat" equivalent to the verbal command *"PLAY!"*; he then brings the baton down across the body on the first beat of the march and continues to beat time. *If he faces the band* while he gives these signals, *the band remains at the halt while playing,* and does not mark time.

The signal to play should consume *one full beat;* the band director may assist the drum major in developing this movement, in order that the band will understand it and will start playing together.

Drum majors use various movements in beating time, but it would seem that the simplest and clearest movement would have the most reasonable military appearance. The first beat of each measure should find the ball of the baton toward the left side of the body no lower than waist level; on the second beat the ball of the baton should be almost directly in front of the right shoulder. The baton should be pointed up and sidewise at the angle of the line between these two points, and should travel approximately in that line, with a slight natural rebound at the end of the first beat. The positions of the baton for this method of beating time are shown in Figs. 38 and 39.

Fig. 38
First Beat

Fig. 39
Second Beat

To discontinue playing, the drum major twirls the baton with a long whistle, raises the baton over his shoulder at arm's length pointing up and slightly to the right, blows a few more long whistles in rapid succession until he is sure he has the band's attention, allows a considerable pause after the last long whistle, then brings the baton down across the body with a short whistle on the last note to be played. The signal should be started from *eight to sixteen measures* before the band is to stop playing, to give the players ample warning. They must continue to play, however, with full volume, until the final signal is given. The band must be prepared to stop playing at the middle or end of any strain, or at any other place the drum major may give this signal; if he does not give it at the end of the march, they should begin to play it again from the beginning. The drum major must always indicate when the band is to cease playing as well as when it is to start playing. The instruments are lowered to the carry positions as soon as the playing has ceased.

The drum major should usually blow more than one long whistle with any preparatory signal while the band is playing, but should always allow a pause after the last one in order to make the signal of execution stand out by itself, clearly. It is possible to execute any logical movement for which there is a drum major's signal, while the band is playing, but the members must be given time to comprehend the preparatory signal before the signal of execution is thrust upon them.

By special command the band may be instructed to mark time while playing, to help bridge the difference between playing while standing still and playing while marching.

The band director should use good judgment in choosing the numbers to be played on the march. They should be solidly built and full sounding, to give the band good volume and confidence in itself; all parts should be clearly defined, and not too difficult; especially there should be a good trombone part, containing lots of melody or countermelody. If the second and third trombone parts are not of particular harmonic importance, all may play the first part to secure uniform slide positions. As a general rule concert marches do not go well on the march; the band should not be expected to play while marching as difficult numbers as they play in concert. Not many numbers need be used in one season for marching, so they may be chosen with particular care.

All players must have music lyres and march folios, and be required to use them, both for the sake of uniform appearance and for the music itself. Many players think they need not carry music because they know their parts, but they will be the first ones to make mistakes in repeats and endings, and many times will fail to "come through" in weak spots. Even if they do know their parts, it will do them no harm to have the music up for reference. These remarks do not apply if the entire band has memorized the music, and is instructed not to carry music.

To announce a number to be played while on the march, all the drum major or director should do is to give the title or number of the march to the man on the right of the front rank. All players in the first file relay this information first to the man to the rear, then to the man on the left; all other players relay it only to the person on the left. This must be done distinctly but quietly, with the least possible disturbance. This procedure may be practiced at the halt, and timed to see how quickly the player on the rear left corner of the band gets the information from the proper source. Each player is responsible for seeing that the "thread" is not broken at any point.

EXERCISE 18. STARTING TO PLAY AND STARTING TO MARCH

If the drum major *faces away from the band* while giving the signals for the raise of instruments and for starting to play, *the band begins to march* with the first beat of the music, stepping off with a full step on the left foot.

Individual players should practice playing and marching at home, to familiarize themselves with the conditions and the music, before the entire band tries it together. It may take some time before the band plays as well on the march as in standing or sitting still, but practice makes perfect, and the band should try to make the marches sound exactly the same in all respects, whether in marching or concert formation. Good volume is a great asset to the marching band, but if the band plays in good rhythm and solidly, with the long tones well sustained and the short tones brilliant through proper breath control, power will soon develop. The drums need not predominate, but their playing must be unusually precise.

It will be found that if the players bend their knees well in marching, and will let the toe strike the ground slightly before the heel, there will be less jar on the body than with the heel striking first; consequently it will be easier to play the instrument well. It is a little harder physically over a period of time, so it is not practical to march in this way while not playing; however, it is well worth the effort for both appearance and playing results, if the entire band will march in this manner while playing.

When the band is marching without playing, the drum major's "step" is the same as that of the individual player. When he is marching and beating time for playing, the manner of step may vary from that recommended in the preceding paragraph for the individual player to some degree of the "strut", depending upon the nature of the occasion. For a strictly military parade there should be very little, if any, suggestion of the strut; on a football or pep parade the strut is proper to a degree, *so long as the drum major does not lose his dignity as commanding officer of the band.* The strut should always retain a *military character* proper to the *military march,* and not be made ridiculous by the use of a dance step, as though the drum major were followed by a jazz band.

For the strut in the military mode, the drum major bends the body backward, with the chin well down and in; brings the knee well up with each step until the upper part of the leg is approximately horizontal; and straightens the leg as he places the foot on the ground carefully and easily, with the toe touching slightly before the heel, the foot pointing straight ahead. He must use all the grace and poise he can command, carrying the body from the hips up smoothly and on a level, neither swaying to right or left, nor swinging up and down. He must always use good, conservative judgment in his appearance while marching; *it is always better to underdo than to overdo the strut.*

The drum major never brings his baton to the carry position under the arm while the band is playing. He must always beat time unless he is giving signals for maneuvers of the band. There are times when he may perform theatrical twirling manipulations with the baton; this will be spoken of later.

EXERCISE 19. STARTING TO PLAY WHILE MARCHING

The usual manner of starting to play while on the march makes use of the "roll-off" drum figure. The drum major gives the preparatory signal for the raise of instruments; the drums then finish the marching figure they are playing, and follow it immediately with the "roll-off" figure as given in Fig. 40. On the fifth beat of this figure the drum major raises the instruments with the baton signal; on the last (silent) beat of the figure he gives the signal *"PLAY!"*, and the band plays the first note on the next beat, assuming that all marches used begin or are made to begin on the "down beat".

Fig. 40

The "roll-off" method of announcing that the band is about to play is not approved by some band directors, who prefer that the band begin playing almost without announcement. In this case, a cymbal crash is inserted on the beat where the roll-off ordinarily would begin, and the drums play one more marching figure. The raise of instruments and the signal for starting to play take place exactly as in the first method. The cymbal player must be trained *never to miss* that single crash, if the latter method is to be used.

EXERCISE 20. HALT WHILE PLAYING

The drum major gives the signals for this halt as though the band were marching with neither music nor the regular drum marching figure. However, if desired, at the preparatory signal the field drums may leave their actual music to begin a continuous, loud roll to better attract the attention of the band members, end the roll on the signal of execution, and succeed it with single strokes on the next two beats, indicating the two counts used in the halt; they resume the regular music for the piece on the next "down beat".

The halt while playing is quite difficult to do precisely, but it may be helped tremendously by the above method, or by having the drum major give the signal of execution at a logical place in the music, such as the fourth beat from the end of any strain, or the first beat of the seventh measure of any of the usual eight measure phrases.

The band must be reminded not to confuse the signals for *Ceasing to Play* and for the *Halt*. *Neither implies the other*. The playing must not weaken when the halt signal is given, neither should any member stop marching at the signal to cease playing.

EXERCISE 21. FORWARD MARCH WHILE PLAYING

If the band is playing at the halt or while marking time, the signal of execution for the *Forward March* must be given on the *second beat* of a measure, which corresponds to the *right foot* in marching. It should occur on the last beat of a strain in the music, or on the second beat of the last measure of one of the phrases, to make it as natural as possible for the band to step off together. The long drum roll may be made use of as in Exercise 20, omitting the last two beats, if desired.

The band must be trained to step out with a full step on the first beat after the signal under any conditions. Many times this seemingly simple movement will win as much appreciation from the spectator as an intricate formation. In special formation work the signal for *Forward March* is often given while the band is marking time and playing, although in street parades, if the band is forced to slow down to the mark time, no signal need be given to resume the march, except the drum major himself stepping off.

THE TRAINING PROGRAM

Unit VI

OTHER FUNDAMENTAL MOVEMENTS

EXERCISE 22.   DIMINISH FRONT

Command: "Diminish Front—MARCH!"

The *Diminish Front* movement is made to reduce the width of the band from the regular formation to one with a smaller interval. At the command or signal of execution all files close toward the center of the band, *while marching obliquely forward;* all members follow their file leaders, *keeping the files straight* during the maneuver. The front rank especially must practice this, and see that the spaces between the files reduce evenly, not too fast toward the center as is the general tendency. This may be accomplished accurately if each player will keep himself equidistant from the person on each side of him during the movement. When the interval is of the size desired the verbal command *Forward March* may be given, and all movement to the center ceases.

For the preparatory signal for *Diminish Front,* the drum major twirls the baton with the long whistle, faces the band, marching backward, at the same time bringing the ferrule of the baton into the left hand at the left shoulder, and placing the ball of the baton at the right hip; for the signal of execution the baton is raised a few inches at that angle, and lowered again with a short whistle, remaining there during the movement. This position is illustrated in Fig. 41. To resume the forward march, the drum major whips the baton from the above angle to a horizontal position with a short whistle; he then turns about to march forward, bringing the baton to its proper position.

Fig. 41

"Diminish Front—"

EXERCISE 23. INCREASE FRONT

Fig. 42
"Increase Front—"

Command: "Increase Front—
MARCH!"

The movement *Increase Front*
is just the reverse of *Diminish
Front,* increasing the reduced interval not more than to the regular interval. It is executed in a
similar manner. The position of
the baton for the drum major's
signal is also the reverse—the
ferrule of the baton in the left
hand at the left hip, and the ball
of the baton in the right hand at
the right shoulder, as in Fig. 42.

In ordinary street parades these
movements should not be necessary as the marching space varies;
the front rank may be instructed
to use all the available space up to
the width of the regular interval,
changing the interval as necessary, making sure that it remains
even.

EXERCISE 24. RIGHT BY FOURS

Command: "Right by Fours—MARCH!"

A different method of diminishing the front of the band consists
of actually reducing the number of files to one-half, one-third, or
one-fourth their original number, and so on, down to a single file.
This may be done to the center in various ways, or to the right or
left. The movement to either side lends itself more readily to all
file combinations, and is the method recommended and illustrated
here. The files always should be divided evenly to avoid confusion:
eight files may be reduced to four, two, and one; six files to three,
two, and one, etc.

In the *Right by Fours* movement from an original formation of
eight files, executed from the halt, all members of files 1 to 4
mark time, with the drums playing the marching figure, while
members of files 5 to 8 execute a right face on the first two counts,
step forward on the third with the *left foot,* maintaining straight
files by *guiding to the front* of the band, march back of their ranks

and take their places behind numbers 1 to 4, *midway* between the regular ranks, turning to the front as they reach their places. *All mark time* until a subsequent command is given. If the band is marching, the command of execution for *Right by Fours* should be given on the *right foot,* on a silent beat of the drum figure; files 5 to 8 take one more step forward, face to the right in marching and proceed as above, while the rest of the band slows to the *half step* until the maneuver is completed. While marching in the new formation the distance should be just *half the regular distance.* The *Right by Fours* movement is illustrated in Figs. 43 and 44.

Fig. 43	Fig. 44
RIGHT BY FOURS	RIGHT BY FOURS
In Process	The Completed Movement

The band is returned to its original formation by the command 'Band Formation—MARCH!". If the band is at the halt, files 5 to 8 execute a left face and march back into their regular positions, guiding front and turning to the front when in place, the entire band marking time as in the previous movement. If the band is marching, the command of execution should be given on the *left foot;* files 5 to 8 take one more step forward, face to the left in marching, and proceed as above, the rest of the band taking a *half step* until all are in place.

If the command is *Left by Fours,* files 5 to 8 remain in place while files 1 to 4 move to new positions behind the members' respective ranks by a movement similar to those above. Band formation is again resumed by the command to that effect and a movement in the reverse direction.

There are no signals for these commands. It is impractical to execute them while playing, so no baton signals are actually needed. The drum major should face the band while giving the verbal commands, regulating the step if the band is marching. He should have the drums play the marching figure *on the shells,* by the command or signal previously explained, in order that the entire band may hear the commands.

If it is desired to reduce the front of the band to less than half the number of original files, the command, if the band is not already marching, should be in this pattern: *"Right by Twos—Forward—MARCH!"* The right front of the band immediately moves forward at a half step to make room for the additional sets of twos. The distance in any reduced formation of this kind should always be *one-half the regular distance.* The final positions of any rank, by numbers, in the *Right by Twos,* are as follows:

$$
\begin{array}{cc}
2 & 1 \\
4 & 3 \\
6 & 5 \\
8 & 7
\end{array}
$$

At the command, numbers 1 and 2 of the front rank march forward at a half-step; numbers 3 to 8 of all ranks face to the right; numbers 3 to 8 of the front rank then step forward at a full step until they reach their relative positions behind numbers 1 and 2 of their rank, turn to the left and close up to half the regular distance at a full step. When numbers 7 and 8 of the first rank have turned the second time, the second rank proceeds with the same directions as given for the front rank, except that numbers 1 and 2 of this rank close up to the proper distance at a full step. The movement proceeds, *one rank at a time,* until the whole band is in the new formation. *Each rank marks time* until the preceding rank has entirely closed to the right, then moves out—numbers 1 and 2 straight forward, and numbers 3 to 8 straight to the right and then forward. When the entire band is in the new formation it may march at a full step, avoiding "straggling out". At the command *Band Formation* all ranks re-form *at the same time,* with the players marching diagonally to their proper places at a full step, numbers 1 and 2 of all ranks slowing to the half step; *guide* is to the *front* of the band in this movement; as each rank is re-formed it closes up to its regular distance behind the preceding rank.

Sometimes it is desired that the band form a circle and play in this formation. This may be done by giving the command *"Right by File",* meaning "Right by Ones"; the drum major leads the single line into the form of a circle, halts the band when all are placed, and gives the command *Right* or *Left Face* toward the center. To re-form band formation, the players may be faced back in the line of the circle and given *Forward March,* the drum major leading number one of the front rank out in the direction desired, then giving the command *Band Formation.*

All other similar movements to the right or left may be patterned after the examples given above. It will be well worthwhile for the band to know how to execute several of them.

EXERCISE 25. THE RIGHT OBLIQUE
Command: "Right Oblique—MARCH!"

The *Right Oblique* movement is a very quick and direct method for moving the band *diagonally* forward and to the right. If the oblique type of *Column Right* is used, each rank will have had experience in marching in an oblique direction. In the *Right Oblique* movement the entire band moves *together* in that direction. At the command each player takes *one step forward,* turns 45 degrees to the right, and marches with a *full step;* if the band is marching when the command is given, the command of execution should be given on the *right foot.* *Guide* is to the *front* and *right* of the band; if all the intervals and distances are correct, and the

Fig. 45
The RIGHT OBLIQUE

movement is done accurately, each player on the inside and rear of the band may also "cover down" in a diagonal, and march in its line. This movement does not alter the relative positions of the ranks and files or the general shape of the band; it merely causes the band to *move by a corner instead of by the front.* The distinction between this movement and the *Column Half Right* is that in the former *the entire band moves together,* while in the latter the band turns to the new direction *one rank at a time.* The *Right Oblique* is illustrated in Fig. 45.

The band resumes marching in the original direction at the command for *Forward March,* with the command of execution occurring on the *left foot.*

To develop precision in the *Right Oblique,* it is advised that the band be faced in the new direction and properly aligned, then marched in that direction immediately. The movement may then be executed properly from the halt or while marching.

The preparatory signal for the *Right Oblique* consists of twirling the baton with the long whistle, and bringing it to a position at arm's length pointing diagonally to the right and diagonally upward, as shown in Fig. 46. For the signal of execution the drum major pulls the ball of the baton back to the right shoulder and jabs it back in the same direction immediately, with a short whistle; this signal should be given on the *right foot,* if the band is marching, and at a logical or natural place in the drum figure or music, as explained in former cases. To resume the forward march the drum major gives the signal in that direction, *turning to that direction himself on the right foot* before giving the signal of execution on the next beat.

Fig. 46
"Right Oblique—"

It is important that the baton be pointed *exactly diagonally* in the signals for the *oblique* movements, and *exactly horizontally* in the signals for the *turns,* otherwise they cannot be clearly distinguished by the members of the band.

EXERCISE 26.   THE LEFT OBLIQUE

Fig. 47
"Left Oblique—"

Command: "Left Oblique—

MARCH!"

The band executes the *Left Oblique* similarly to the *Right Oblique,* but 45 degrees to the left. If the band is at the halt when the command is given, the first step is in the new direction; if it is marching, the command of execution is given on the *left foot,* the next step is forward, and the second step is in the new direction. The command for *Forward March* from the *Left Oblique* is given on the *right foot.*

The drum major's signal for this movement is similar to that for the *Right Oblique,* except that the baton points to the left, as shown in Fig. 47.

THE TRAINING PROGRAM
Unit VII
THE SALUTES

It is proper for a band in uniform to follow to some extent the military system of salutes. If the band is marching past a reviewing stand, the American flag, another band or organization, or a distinguished personage to whom it is desired to pay tribute, the drum major, representing the band, salutes with his baton. Likewise, if the band is in marching formation, and the flag, person, or group passes by, the drum major brings the band to attention and gives the baton salute.

The position of the baton salute is shown in Fig. 48. To execute the salute, the drum major brings the baton to the carry position, if it is not already there; changes the grip of the right hand on the baton so that the thumb is on top and pointing to the ball; extends the baton, in a vertical position pointing downward, straight out to the right at arm's length; then immediately brings it across his body, in the vertical position, placing the ball of the baton in front of his left shoulder. The drum major turns his head to look in the general direction of the element being saluted. He times the salute so that it will begin five yards before he reaches the line of the element, or when it reaches the same distance in passing him, and will end five yards after it is (or has) passed.

Individual band members in uniform should stand at attention and execute the hand salute if the flag passes by, or the national anthem is being played by another group. If the band is together in concert formation, the same suggestions apply. When the song of another school is being played or sung, however, it is more proper for each player to stand and remove his cap. The position of the hand salute is illustrated in Fig. 49.

The courtesies of the salutes are very impressive and dignified, and every band should take advantage of them.

Fig. 48
The Baton Salute

Fig. 49
The Hand Salute

CONCLUSION OF SECTION I

It is felt that any band perfecting the maneuvers or movements explained in the seven units of the training program outlined above will have an adequate fundamental marching repertoire for all occasions, and will be able to add much to its prestige. Special letter formations and other demonstrations must be worked out separately, but their content will always involve the real fundamentals of the marching band; it is strongly advised that all bands spend as much time as is available on the foundation before attempting the more spectacular top, suggestions for which are contained in the next section of this book.

It will be seen that the successful marching band must be made up of serious students of marching, who will learn the various exercises and signals through diligent study and practice. The student edition of this book, containing short explanations and illustrations of all the above exercises, is available in march folio form, and may easily be carried in the coat pocket or in the music lyre of the instrument on the drill field; it should prove invaluable in the development of the marching band, if along with it the more technical details are furnished by the drillmaster or drum major from their experience and from the contents of this complete edition.

BAND—AT-TEN-TION!

Section II

SPECIAL PARADES AND FORMATIONS

I have repeatedly made the statement that bands should express individuality in their special parades and formations. Straight marching and the fundamental maneuvers in marching are more or less standard, but an attempt to standardize parade programs, especially in large municipalities where there are several bands, or among bands that are seen frequently by the same people, would defeat the purpose of entertainment and the element of surprise for which they are intended. My purpose in writing this section, therefore, is not to lay down a set of rules to be followed in this type of performance; it is rather to express my own ideas on the subject, and to explain several kinds of formations that have been used successfully by various bands, with the hope that they will stimulate other original lines of thought and procedure.

We shall be concerned here only with the "football parade", inasmuch as it is the most common type of "program parade", and furnishes sufficient material that may be used for other occasions. Tastes differ in this case just as they differ in nearly everything else. I make no claim that my ideas are better or even as good as those of other people; I offer them only for what they are worth to band executives who have had less experience along this line.

In my opinion, a good football parade will involve certain points, which I may outline as follows:

1. It must have an impressive beginning, or "entrance".

2. Formations of letters or symbols should proceed rapidly from one to another, using a reasonable amount of straight marching and regular maneuvers, but only to get in proper position for the formations.

3. The parade should be so designed that it pays tribute to all schools represented, both in formations and music.

4. There should be music continuously throughout the parade.

5. It should have an effective close.

The material and procedure for the football parade will be discussed in this section, with the above points in mind.

A. THE ENTRANCE

By the word "entrance" I refer to the beginning of the program parade, and not necessarily to the initial appearance of the band on the field. The object of the entrance is to introduce or announce the band in a manner more effective than just starting to march and play. It usually involves the use of a cornet or trumpet "call" or "flourish", such as is found in the introduction to many marches.

The band is usually formed for the parade at the end of the football field, back of the goal posts, if possible. For the simplest entrance using the trumpet music at the beginning, the band may be in regular formation, starting to play at the end of the "flourish", and starting to march down the field at the same time or at the beginning of the first regular strain of the number. For a variation of this method the trumpets may be placed in front of the band, to take their regular places in the formation as the band marches "through" or past them.

Figs. 50 and 51 illustrate two entrances I have used, involving both the trumpet introduction and irregular formations of the band.

Fig. 50

In the first entrance, the band forms in very close formation as in (1) ; at a whistle signal from the drum major, who is "hidden" within the band, the trumpets march out from both sides and form a line ten yards ahead of the band as shown in (2) ; one field drum has given them the cadence on the drum shell; at a cymbal signal the trumpets raise their instruments and play their flourish; on the last four measures they march out to the positions shown in (3) and the drum major appears ahead of the band; on the first beat of the first strain of the march the band steps out, taking the regular distance immediately, and increasing the front as soon as they have passed the trumpet opening as in (4) ; the trumpets finally march into their places at the rear of the band, and all proceed down the field.

Fig. 51

In the second entrance illustrated, the band forms in two equal parts, in close formation, as in (1) ; at a signal from the drum major, the trumpets and drums march out from each side and take their places as in (2) ; after the trumpet introduction, the band starts playing, and the two sections march together as in (3), with the drums and trumpets going to their regular places as the band marches by. The regular interval and distance are assumed gradually as the band marches out.

In some places the band marches on the field or into the stadium in single or double files from various points, preceded by the drum section or a drum and bugle corps from a central point; the corps furnishes music for the band to get into regular formation, then the drum major appears and the parade begins. Different types of structures will suggest other effective means of bringing the band on the field for a short parade or flag-raising ceremony before the game; usually the program parade itself occurs between the halves of the game.

Entrances ordinarily must be taught to the band "by rote", although in some cases it may be possible to use charts, as suggested later in the letter formations.

B.   Formations "On Location"

The "theory" of all formations may be worked out on "squared" or "graph" paper fastened to a drawing board, using pins with colored heads—a different color head for each kind of instrument or for each rank. Directions for the formation may then be transferred to a form which may be used on the field. Each formation may be taught "by rote", but to save the time of many individuals during the drill period, it is recommended that specific directions be worked out in the office and given each player in advance. One practice is to give each member a card on which only his particular instructions are written. The plan illustrated in this discussion, however, will involve a chart of the whole formation, which may be mimeographed or otherwise duplicated, and on which the movement of any player may be traced with a colored pencil; each player is given the copy which has his movement duplicated by the colored line; he can easily find his place because also on his copy appears the movements and places of the rest of the band members.

Perhaps the simplest method of forming a letter is to make it "on location"—bringing the band into the position desired and forming the letter on and around the spot on which the band is standing. The first letter illustrated will be the very simple *"I"*, using the 88 piece band plus the field officer; the drum major is not usually used in the letter formation; instead, he stands in front or at the side of the letter, depending upon the next movement.

The first thing to do is to determine the design and the proportions of the letter which are possible and practical for the band that is to form the letter. After a series of experiments with pencil and scratch paper, it may be decided that with an 88 piece band, the stem of the letter *"I"* will be 4 men wide and 13 long; each of the "legs" on the four corners of the letter will be 3 x 3; this uses everyone but the field officer, and, for lack of something better, he will have to be inserted in a convenient place where he will not be noticed particularly.

In letter formations of this type the files are usually half the regular interval apart, or one and one-fourth yards. The distance may vary, but should seldom be more than the regular distance. For practical purposes, the distance should be uniform throughout the letter. On the "squared" paper, each line may be taken to represent one yard, or half a yard, on the field; the five-yard lines of the football field in the area where the letter is to be formed may be drawn off and marked. Now the design of the letter as determined above may be drawn on the paper, using a small circle to represent the position of each player in the letter. The pins with the colored heads may now be stuck through the paper and into the drawing board, to represent the regular marching formation of the band immediately before the letter is to be formed. This procedure will result in a diagram or picture such as Fig. 52. From this the decisions may be made as to the movements of the various players to get into the letter formation, and the pins transferred to the circles. At the same time a record of these movements should be made on a "master chart" for later duplication.

In the "working" charts, each band member is given the number corresponding to his place in the regular marching formation, as explained in the first paragraph on the "Marching Formation" in Section I. The figures in the chart represent the original formation of the band; the circles represent the positions of the players in the letter formation. If there is a circle around a number, it indicates the player is to stand fast—unless there is also a cross (X) in the circle, which means that he moves elsewhere and his place is taken by another. It is usually best for as many players to stand fast as possible, but the instruments must be kept in mind, and placed advantageously for the best appearance and musical results. The lines from the numbers to the circles indicate the approximate movements of the players to their new positions; they should always "guide" and "cover" whenever possible in getting to their places. It is recommended that in the ordinary formation "on location" there be only one signal for the letter, each man going directly to his place by the simplest and quickest movement, avoiding various "sub-formations" which call for additional signals and movements. The return to band formation may be accomplished by an exactly reverse movement. The proper yard-lines should appear on the chart, to establish correct proportions and definite locations. Usually

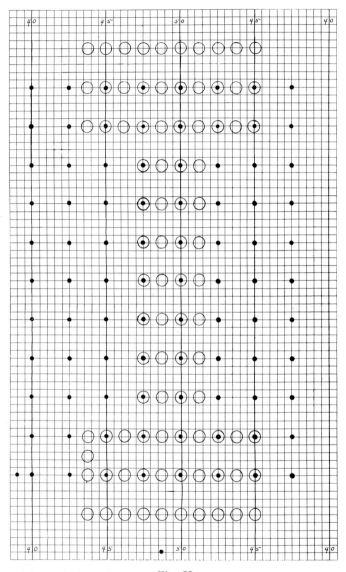

Fig. 52

the base of the letter should be at the top of the page; an arrow should indicate the direction the players are to face in the completed letter.

A copy of the completed chart should be provided each member of the band; before they are distributed, however, each copy must be marked *in color* with the particular player's number, his movement traced, and his final position indicated by "filling in" his circle. It will be found convenient to have on hand mimeographed copies of the regular band formation by numbers, to facilitate making up the original chart of each formation "on location".

The sample chart in Fig. 54 will illustrate the formation of the letter "*I*" with the minimum movement from the regular marching formation; Fig. 55 will show the same formation with more movement, but designed for better appearance as to the instruments; Fig. 56 will illustrate the same letter on the same location, but with the band originally facing "down the field", instead of "across the field". The completed letter will appear as in Fig. 53, according to the directions of the chart in Fig. 55.

Fig. 53

_____BAND

1932

"*I*" Formation

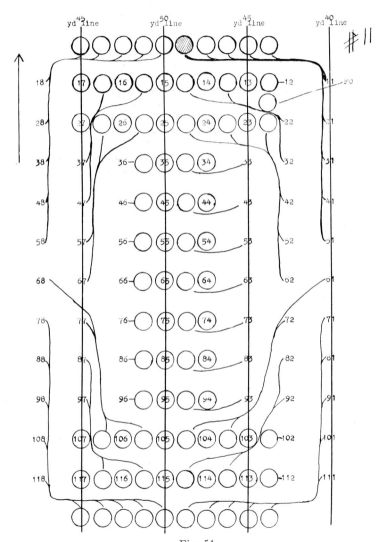

Fig. 54

BAND

1932

"*T*" Formation

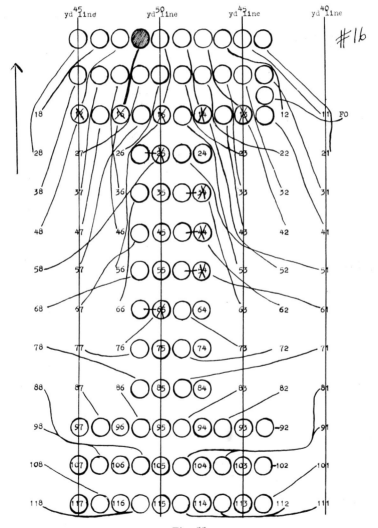

Fig. 55

_____BAND

1932

"*I*" Formation

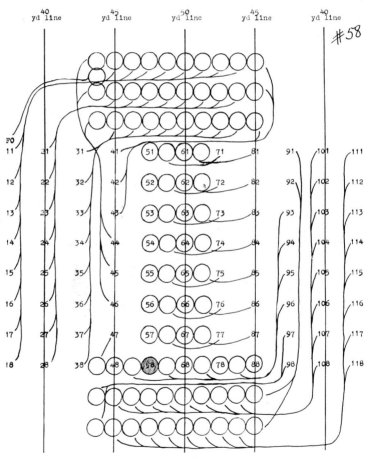

Fig. 56

The next formation will illustrate the use of single and double file letters, in the combination "*H H S*". When one band forms all the letters at the same time, three separate charts are necessary. Small bands may follow the directions and suggestions in each of the charts for forming the letters singly. Fig. 57 shows the completed formation; Figs. 58 to 60 are charts from which the formation is derived. Note the width and height of the letters, and the space between them.

Fig. 57

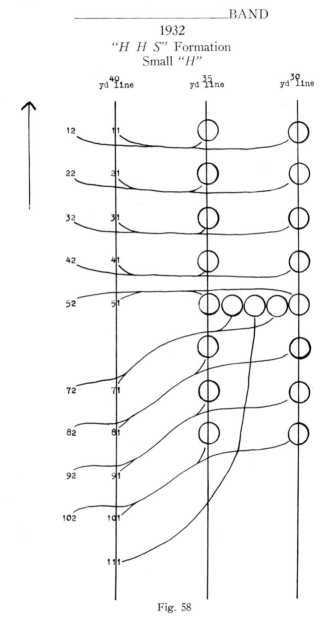

_____BAND

1932
"H H S" Formation
Small "H"

Fig. 58

_____BAND

1932
"H H S" Formation
Large "H"

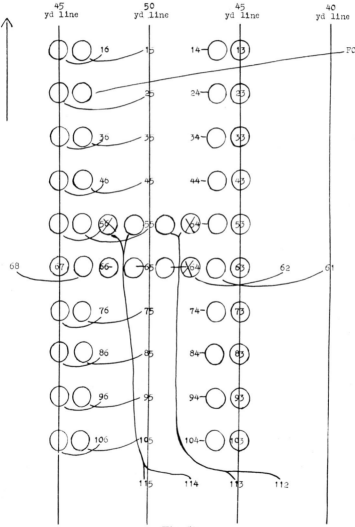

Fig. 59

_____BAND

1932
"*H H S*" Formation
"*S*"

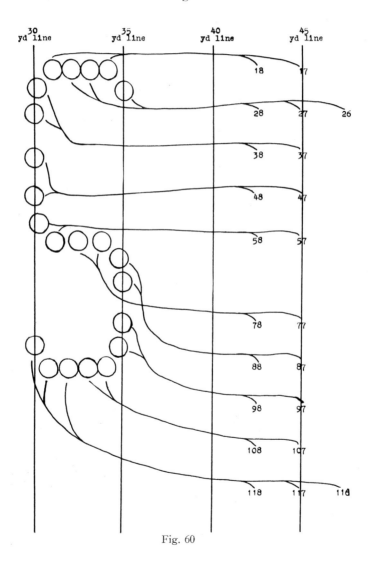

Fig. 60

Sometimes the band may wish to spell out the name of a school, or a coach, or a visitor. This may be done effectively by dividing the band into small "blocks"—one for each letter, marching each block to its proper location, then at a signal forming all the letters simultaneously. Fig. 61 demonstrates this type of formation, showing first the blocks, then the complete word *"ARMY"*.

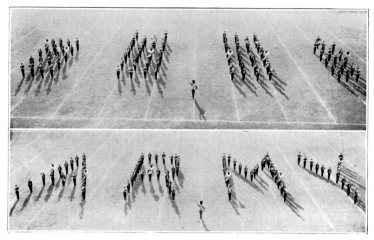

Fig. 61

The school monogram often offers an interesting design for bands to copy. The monogram may be made in one movement, or the letters may be formed singly, then marched together. Figs. 62 and 63 illustrate monograms derived from the letters *"I U"* and *"H H S"*.

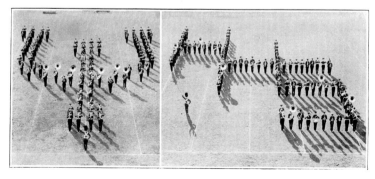

Fig. 62   Fig. 63

Certain emblems lend themselves readily to formations by the band. Since we are thinking primarily in terms of the football parade, the *football* itself may be used as an example. It is illustrated in Fig 64. An interesting result is obtained if the "ovals" in the football are made to revolve in opposite directions, indicating the "turmoil" of a football game. When this formation was used, the football finally "unwound" at both ends, the players leading off into a number of small blocks, from which letters representing the visiting school were made. Many other ideas in the use of characteristic figures and emblems will probably suggest themselves.

Fig. 64

C. "Moving" Formations

Somewhat more advanced and more interesting than formations "on location" are the "moving" formations, in which the letters are formed while the band is marching, with the letters continuing to move down the field, probably changing to other letters on the way. An example of this type is the "*H A R V A R D*" formation made by the Indiana University Band in the Harvard stadium in 1927. The entire band formed each letter in the name "*HARVARD*" while marching the length of the field, going from one letter directly into the next as soon as each was formed. Fig. 65 is a composite photograph of that performance, showing each letter on the ground where it was made.

Movements of this kind should be taught to the band as though it were to remain "on location" to form all the letters; in fact, this in itself would make an interesting performance. Charts may be made in the regular way, except that the starting position for the "*A*" will be the "*H*", and the starting position for the "*R*" will be the "*A*", etc. These charts will be more difficult to make clearly than those in which the letters are made from the regular marching formation. After the letters are worked out by the band "on location", they may be made while marching, almost by the trial and error process, until the timing, guiding, and placing of all members are accomplished smoothly. A very slow cadence and a very short step must be used at first to avoid many mishaps. The letters must move from the spectator's left to right for the proper picture. The charts in Figs. 66 and 67 illustrate how the first two letters in "*HARVARD*" may be formed on location.

INDIANA UNIVERSITY BAND
1927
"H A R V A R D" Formation
"H"

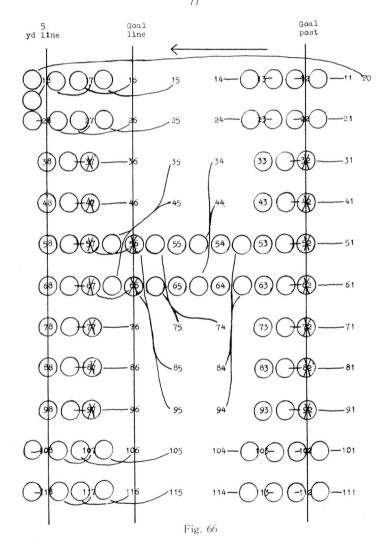

Fig. 66

INDIANA UNIVERSITY BAND
1927
"*H A R V A R D*" Formation
First "*A*"

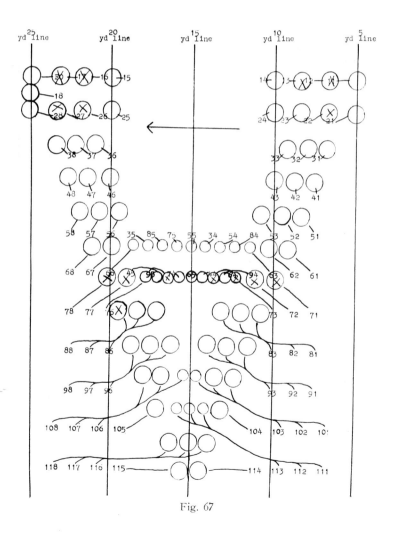

Fig. 67

Another type of moving formation is patterned after the moving "electric sign". Single letters move out of the regular band formation, one after another, proceed down the field from the spectator's right to left, and finally disappear into a new band formation at the other end of the field. Fig. 68 shows this method of spelling the word *"PURDUE"*, first in the early stages, then in the completed formation, then in returning to the regular marching formation.

Fig. 68

_____BAND

1932

"*P U R D U E*" Formation

"*P*"

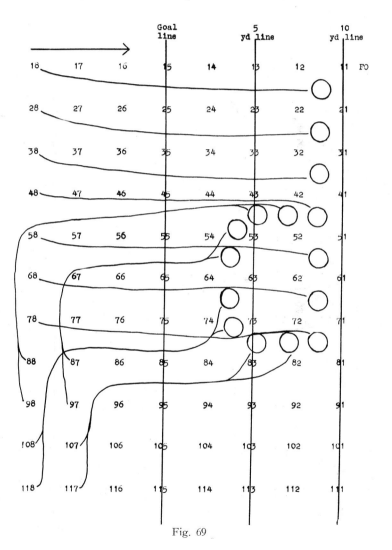

Fig. 69

_____BAND

1932
"*P U R D U E*" Formation
First "*U*"

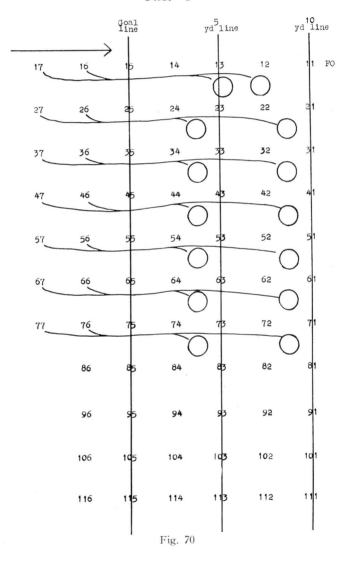

Fig. 70

For the first letter, players from the "far" side of the band are chosen; they march through the remainder of the band, forming the letter "P" on the way, so that when they emerge from the band the letter will be shaped. Succeeding letters are formed in similar manner, until by the time the letter "E" is made every player has been used. At the other end of the field, the letter "P" breaks up and starts the regular formation, the other letters marching through the players thus formed and into their regular places, completing the movement.

For a formation of this kind it is best to make charts for each letter involving only the players actually used in each, omitting the movements of the rest of the band. This will at least show them their relative positions, even though it does not indicate the entire movement. Since, however, the number of players in each letter is comparatively small, the drillmaster may wish to teach the band this formation from an original chart he has made up, without taking the time to cut stencils for duplication. Figs. 69 and 70 suggest the type of chart for the first two letters in "PURDUE".

D.   THE COMPLETED PARADE

The plan of the program parade must be very definite, and must be thoroughly worked out in advance of the performance; every movement and every formation must have a specific time and place. Nothing should be left to the last-minute discretion of the drum major or field officer. It is only in this way that every band member will know just what to do in every situation. It is also very important that the parade be timed to fit the space allotted for it.

The special formations desired will often suggest the general plan of the parade. The band at some time should cover almost the entire length of the field, but the formations themselves should occur near the center of the field, toward the side to which they are presented. An outline of the parade may be sketched on a miniature design of the football field, to get it well in mind.

The first formation usually occurs when the band reaches the center of the field after the entrance. It may be one which applies to both schools, or to the school which the band represents. After this the band may be maneuvered toward the stands of the opposite school for formations and music which are appropriate. The tribute to the band's own school may conclude the parade on the other side of the field. After the parade proper, the band may remain in the position of the last formation for the playing and singing of the alma mater song by the band and student body, if desired; very often the band may effectively sing a part of the song by itself, with or without accompaniment by a few members of the band. After the conclusion the band may be brought into regular formation and marched directly to their seats as quickly and quietly as possible.

The band should never remain in one formation for too long a time—never over half a minute, except possibly in the last one. The sparkle and continuity of the parade will be more effective if the band marks time when not marching; this will also make possible better alignment of the letters.

Signals for the regular marching maneuvers of the band should be given by the drum major; it is also possible for him to indicate the special formations by prearranged special signals, if this is desired. Some bands are instructed to halt at certain yard lines on the football field, and then to make the formation at a definite place in the music. I prefer usually that the formation take place immediately the band has reached the proper position; the movement within and from the formation may then be made according to the music; this will alleviate the probability of long waits or unnecessary hurrying before the time of the formation. I have also found that pistol shots for all signals which the drum major cannot give in regular marching routine produce more precise movements than those by other methods. The response of the band to the pistol signal is always immediate, and the close attention of the spectator is called for and more easily kept. I do not believe that pistol shots, properly used, detract from the music of the parade; on the contrary, it adds an edge to the performance which is quite attractive to the average spectator. These signals may be given both for the location of the formation and for timing it with the music. For a large band, the pistol should be of .32 or .38 caliber. If the signals are numerous, more than one pistol must be carried, or ample time allowed for reloading with blank cartridges.

The average parade of six to eight minutes in length will usually require all or parts of two marches in addition to the marching songs of the two schools. These numbers need not be played in regular order, but may be woven together in strains or trios to fit the parade. It must be done so as to sound well, but very often all the music is in related keys, and it is possible to go from one number to the next without any bad effects. If the keys are not closely enough related, the transition may be made by omittting the last beat or three beats of one number, either leaving them silent or substituting sufficient modulatory chords or passages to the next number. Usually the band director will not have much difficulty in establishing the proper continuity of the music.

It is advised that each band member be required to memorize the music used in the program parade, so as not to take any time from his marching for reading the music. The band will have a much better appearance if all eyes are free for the marching maneuvers and formations, and the music itself will sound better because of the necessary familiarity of the players with it. Because of the usual limited time available for marching practice, and the intricacy of the program parade, it is recommended that the same general parade be used during one entire season, changing each time only the formation and music for the opposite school; so when once the music is memorized it will be used many times, making necessary only a small amount of new memory work each week. Of course the band will not usually be able to stage the full parade at the first game of the season, but parts of it may be added as they are developed until the complete parade is ready for performance. The spectators will not tire of seeing a good parade throughout an entire season, especially if it enlarges and improves toward the end of the season as it should.

The parade music may be developed to a great extent in the rehearsal room, in connection with blackboard illustrations and signal discussions. The connections between the numbers and the proper times to change from one to another are the important points to rehearse there. As stated before, I believe that the music should be continuous from the entrance to the last formation of the parade; but there should be no doubt in the minds of the players as to the order of the music, and no hesitancy in carrying it

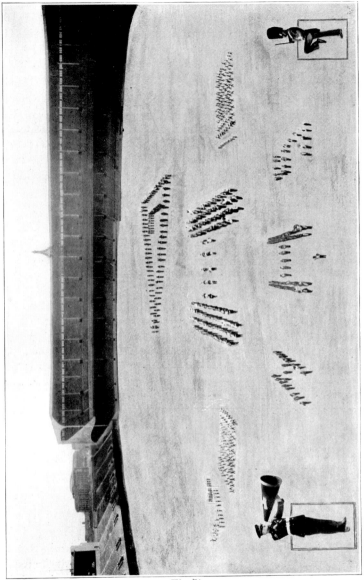

Fig 71

The instruction sheet to be issued to each member of the band for this parade follows.

through. The playing endurance of the band members will soon develop to a point where they can play during the entire parade without undue fatigue of their embouchures; if anyone does stop for rest, however, he must keep his instrument in its playing position for the sake of appearance.

Sometimes the drum major is able to add much to the spectacular side of the parade performance by his ability in fancy twirling of the baton. However, this is only proper and necessary when the band has "nothing to say". The drum major may twirl while the band is marching from the position of one formation to another, and perhaps during the last few seconds of each special formation, but at no time should he deliberately attract the attention of the crowd away from a formation which the entire band may have spent hours to perfect. If he possesses unusual ability which cannot be done justice in this manner, it should be perfectly proper for him to take the field at another time, while the band is playing in concert formation on the sidelines, to entertain the crowd with his stunts. The ability to twirl may be developed by practice under the tutelage of an experienced drum major, or through a study of the subject in drum major's manuals or special articles.

In addition to charts for the various formations, each member should have available for study explicit instructions as to the order of the parade, order of the music, and what to do at every signal. These instructions may be written on the blackboard while they are tentative or only partly developed, and mimeographed as soon as they are permanent. To illustrate this instruction sheet, I will use as an example a parade which I recently used. Fig. 71 is a composite picture of that parade. The order of main events was as follows:

(1) Entrance.

(2) Block *"H"* formation, by a series of maneuvers dividing the band into halves, then fourths, then marching the band back together to form the *"H"*, the drum rank remaining in the center of the field to form the cross-bar. The movement back into band formation was accomplished in a reverse manner. These maneuvers were taught almost entirely by rote.

(3) "Square and Block" formation (not shown), preparatory to the "Pennant and Letter" formation for the opposite school.

(4) *"H H S"* formation.

HEIGHTS HIGH SCHOOL BAND
Parade Instructions, 1931

SIGNALS	FORMATIONS (Movements)	MUSIC
D. M......	Entrance	Intro., Entry of the Heralds.
D. M......	Increase Front..........	E Pluribus Unum to trio, repeating 2nd strain over and over if necessary.
Shot No. 1..	Block H—40 yd. line....	
Shot No. 2..	Drums march into cross-bar; band turns at side-lines.	
Shot No. 3..	Face "far" end of field...	Trio, On Wisconsin.
Shot No. 4..	Right Face............	1st beat, 7th m.
Shot No. 5..	Right Face............	1st beat, 15th m.
Shot No. 6..	Right Face............	1st beat, 23rd m.
Shot No. 7..	Face original direction in H, forward march, return to band formation.	1st beat, 31st m. Trio, E Pluribus Unum (without intro.). Return to beginning of march at end of trio.
D. M......	Countermarch, 10 yd. line.	
D. M......	Right Oblique.	
D. M......	Forward March—5 yds. from sidelines.	
D. M......	Countermarch — 15 yard line.	
Shot No. 8..	Square and Block, immediately after countermarch. Continue to march.....	Trio, Our Director, (without intro.) at end of next strain E P U. Repeat if necessary.
Shot No. 9..	Pennant and Letter. Front rank on 40 yd. line across 50 yd. line.	
Shot No. 10.	Band formation.........	1st beat, 15th m.
Shot No. 11.	Block turn—face Heights stands	1st beat, 31st m. On Wisconsin—entire march, without repeating 2nd strain —2nd beat, 8th m. of first strain, 2nd time.
D. M......	Forward March	

Fig. 72

Fig. 72—(Continued)

Shot No. 12.   HHS formation—5 yds.
                from sidelines.

D. M.....   Cease playing and mark-   —end of On Wiscon-
               ing time.............   sin.
Director ...   Alma Mater.
                                            Reeds play 1st 8 m.
                                            of 1st verse, entire
                                            band remainder; en-
                                            tire band sings 1st
                                            8 m. 2nd verse,
D. M......   Band Formation (drums   play remainder.
               on shells).
D. M......   Right by Fours.
D. M......   Forward March.   March
               into seats and
D. M......   Halt.

No doubt very much remains to be said concerning this special
topic of parades and formations. Many unforeseen conditions arise
in the development of the parade which call for original solution.
Mastery of these situations comes only with experience in meet-
ing them. It is only hoped that these suggestions and illustrations
will give many bands greater ambitions for marching performances,
and will in some measure point the way toward their realization.

Marching Maneuver Series
UP TO THE MINUTE STUNTS
Adaptable to Various Sized Units

VOLUME I

24 Formations, Designs and Entrances

FOR MARCHING BANDS
By MARK H. HINDSLEY
(University of Illinois)

GAMBLE HINGED MUSIC CO. CHICAGO

A Bag of Tricks
for the
Marching Band

CONTENTS
Introduction—Formation Technique

VOLUME II

Practical Stunts and Evolutions

FOR BANDS AND DRUM CORPS
Designed for Smaller Groups
By CLAUDE SMITH and WALLACE CAPEL
(Evansville, Indiana—State Contest Winners for Three Consecutive Years)

CONTENTS
Introduction

STEAL
THE SHOW
WITH THESE
NEW
MARCHING
STUNTS!

Your Band Really Needs These Books—$1.00 Each

GAMBLE HINGED MUSIC CO., Chicago